Put the Baby
Back
in my Tummy

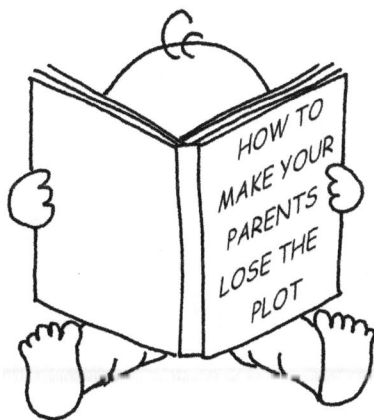

HOW TO MAKE YOUR PARENTS LOSE THE PLOT

Put the Baby
Back
in my Tummy

When Parenthood is Not

Quite as Expected

Anna Garcia

Destined 2 Shine

For permission requests, write to the publisher at the address below:
Destined 2 Shine
1/24 Etonville Parade
Croydon, NSW, 2032, Australia
anna@valuelifecoaching.com
www.putthebabyback.com www.valuelifecoaching.com

The author of this book does not dispense medical advice or prescribe the use of any technique as a form of treatment for physical, emotional, or medical problems without the advice of a physician, either directly or indirectly. The intent of the author is only to offer information of a general nature to help new parents on their parenting journey.
In the event you use any of the information in this book for yourself, which is your right, the author and the publisher assume no responsibility for your actions.
The author has tried to recreate events, locales, and conversations from memories. In order to maintain their anonymity, in some instances the author has changed the names of individuals. Any trademarks or product names are assumed to be the property of their respective owners, and are used only for reference. There is no implied endorsement.

The author would like to acknowledge Hay House Australia Pty Ltd and Dr. John F. Demartini for granting permission to reprint cited material. Inspired Destiny: Living a Fulfilling and Purposeful Life. Reprinted by permission of Dr. John. F. Demartini. © 2013 John F. Demartini

Cover design by Anna Garcia
Illustrations by Anna Garcia
Edited by Jill Slack, www.jillslackediting.com
Photography by In Character Images Pty Ltd

Available from www.amazon.com and other retailers.

1. Parenting 2. Self-help Techniques 3. Humor
Printed in the United States of America.
U.S. Edition, June, 2013

ISBN 978-0-9874824-0-2

Dedication

To Allegra: Thank you for teaching me that the "golden arches" stood for Old Macdonald. You make me want to pull my hair out every day, and smother you with kisses at the same time. I will forever wonder what you will do next.

To Sheldon: Even though you liken our marriage to an onion – the deeper you go in, the more it stings your eyes – I love you immensely. You are an excellent father.

To all my family, friends, health professionals, day care teachers, and volunteers: Thank you for getting me through the toughest times along the journey.

Finally, to all parents who have experienced a not-so-perfect, tumultuous parenting journey: This book is dedicated to you.

Contents

Introduction

This is a story about a quirky little girl and two clueless parents trying to get along in the world. Rather than a love story, it's a falling-in-love story, where the characters don't initially get along; rather battle each other to death, falling in love by the closing credits. It's Shakespeare's play, "Taming of the Shrew," adapted to the parent world, rather than the moving "Romeo and Juliet."

So what inspired me to share this journey with you? It all started a year ago.

There I was, sitting in a photography studio, carrying out my daily routine when a flustered mother stumbled through the door. In one arm she pushed a stroller loaded with all her baby paraphernalia and a baby, while in the other arm, whatever she could throw hastily in her bag walking out the door.

It was a scene I was all too familiar with. Working part-time in a photography studio for babies, it was a common occurrence to see strollers, sleepless moms and dads, seemingly innocent babies, and hearing those inevitable screams. Of course, I was immune to the baby scream. In two years of working here, I managed to put up an invisible force field between myself and their sound waves.

"First baby?" I asked, sitting casually at my desk.

"Yes," she answered.

My automated response for all new mothers rolled out. "Isn't it a shocker?"

That got the ball rolling. Next thing I knew, she was telling me about the enormous challenges she faced bringing up her first baby all on her own while her husband was away serving in the army. She elaborated on the strategies she put in place when the baby just wouldn't stop screaming and the wonderful remedy when all else failed – ignoring it and taking a nice, hot shower!

However, it was her succeeding words that really struck a chord within me. Reflecting upon reading all the self-help books available for new mothers, she despondently pointed out, "It's almost like there's a missing chapter. Every book tells you what to expect, but they don't tell you about this."

Those words resonated within my soul. I completely identified. Giving birth was hard, but raising a baby was even harder and the most challenging experience of my life. It sent me back in time to "those" experiences.

"Put the baby back in my tummy" were the exact words I thought when my daughter Allegra entered the world. I remember feeling guilt and shame at the time because not many people talked about these feelings openly.

During this time of great desperation with my first baby, I could not find much reading material that could help me. Just knowing other mothers had a similar experience would enable me to live through the biggest transition of my life.

I later read a line from an inspirational book "Inspired Destiny" by Dr. John Demartini:

> "*Whatever you perceive as your greatest challenge – whatever you think stops you from living your purpose – may be the very thing you need to achieve your inspired destiny.*"[1]

1. Demartini, John F. *Inspired Destiny: Living a Fulfilling and Purposeful Life.* Carlsbad, CA: Hay House, Inc., 2010.

I was not going to let this be another "tough experience in my past" buried away. There had to be a reason I experienced this. There was something I had learned. So I was inspired to write this book. To let men and women know they weren't alone.

This book is comprised of three parts. If you want to know how the diva journey began, read Part 1: "Memoirs of a Diva." If you have just woken up to the reality that parenthood is not entirely a bed of roses, Part 2: "Parent Survival Kit" has plenty of tips to keep you sane. Finally, Part 3 is something I put together purely for your enjoyment, Allegra's Greatest Hits.

During my journey, a major turning point was when I studied and became a life coach. I began applying some of the strategies I was suggesting to clients and noticed a world of difference in my parenting experience. This must have been the "falling in love" part of the story. I share these strategies in Chapter 15. If you have any questions about how to apply them, you can contact me through anna@valuelifecoaching.com. You can also receive free bonus parenting affirmations by clicking on www.putthebabyback.com. For anyone that wants to know more about my coaching service, you are welcome to visit my website www.valuelifecoaching.com.

I have also included stories from parents all over the world, and the tips they implemented that helped them along the way. I am extremely grateful to all the parents who contributed their tips, even if the suggestion was merely to hide in the pantry.

Of course, "Put the Baby Back in My Tummy" is not meant to replace medical advice and professional advice, diagnosis, or treatment. If you have any feelings of depression or feel you are struggling, see your doctor or local health professional immediately. They can refer you to great services. I sought professional help along the way and highly recommend it. It's okay to ask for help.

Finally, I wrote this book to bring laughter to the soul. After sharing many of my daughters' quirky stories with the world, people started asking me, "Anna, when are you going to write a book?"

I had never written a book and wasn't planning to. Eventually, even friends of day care teachers, wanted to meet the star of these strange stories. I finally came to grips that not sharing her stories would be a punishable crime.

Like jumping into a deep ocean, I immersed myself in every resource and course to deliver my message. As the events were so vivid in my mind and the fullness of Allegra's personality and facial expressions were beyond words, I also decided to illustrate it. So here it is, in written and illustrative form, for you to enjoy.

I hope sharing my experience, tips that helped me, and the light-hearted side of my daughter's personality will help mothers and fathers all over the world with their rite of passage into parenthood.

For every other person who has decided to pick up this book, I hope it gives you something to smile about.

PART I

Memoirs of a Diva

Let's get started

I'd like you to meet Sheldon.
Exhibit A.

He is the father.
And Part A of the equation which would
lead to our little "phenomenon."

Meet Anna.

Exhibit B.

That's me! I'm part B of the equation and the
other contributor to our little one.
As you can see, I'm quite a sophisticated mommy.

Meet Allegra.
Exhibit C.

This cheeky monkey is the result of me
and Sheldon in this equation.
Or should I say an inequation?

Back in school I learned that $1 + 1 = 2$.
In this case, $1+1 = 50$.

You see, Allegra is nothing like us.
She has more character, angst, drama, passion,
independence, and confidence than
Sheldon and I combined.
She is a huge character in a little form and
the reason I can write this story.

So in order to share this story about Allegra and our experience
of first-time parenthood, we need to rewind to before it all began.

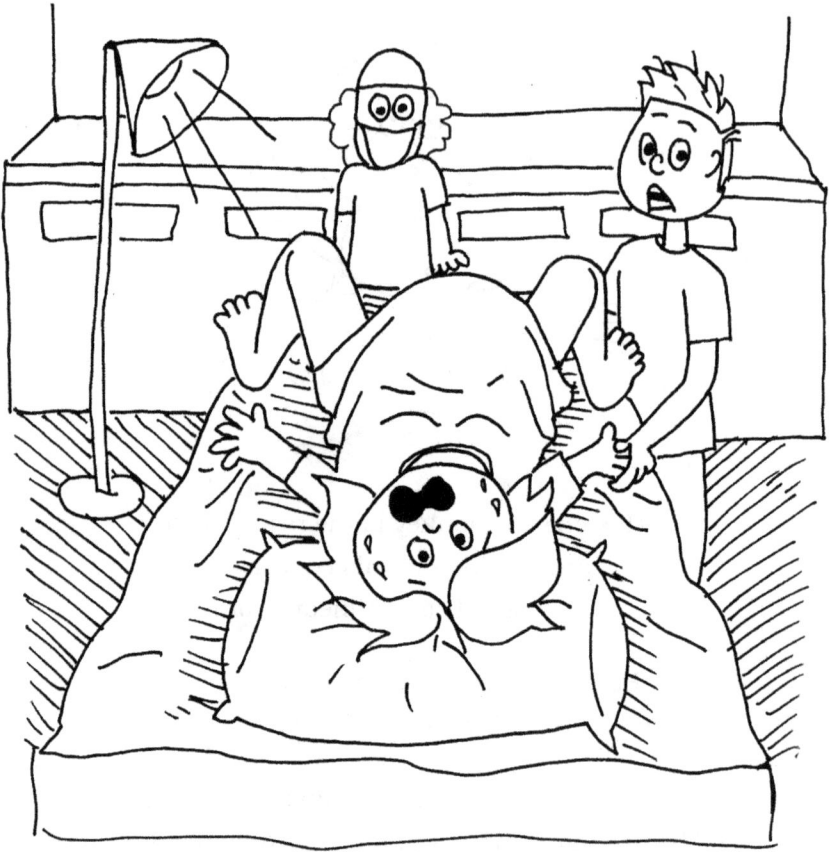

The day Allegra entered the world?

Keep rewinding to the beginning
way before Allegra was born.

To the days when Sheldon and I used to have fun?

Keep rewinding a little further...

Water rafting in Thailand

When muscles were used for adventure instead of carrying
a baby, diapers, and a ton of baby luggage?

Keep rewinding.

When we used to have a designer home where we could actually see the floor and walk injury-free? When everything was color coordinated without spills, tears, or texter marks?

Just a little bit further...

When Sheldon and I used to be in love and had plenty of special date nights? When we could actually taste the food we were eating, and going to the movies wasn't an annual event?

Getting closer. Keep rewinding...

.

Plenty of action

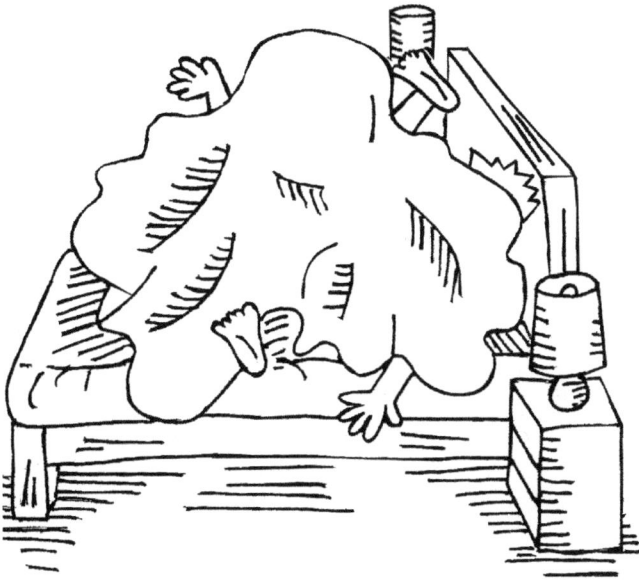

When action occurred in the bedroom
more than once every six months?

Now we are getting closer.

This is it. This is where the story begins.

Chapter 1

4 Years B.D. - 'Before the Diva'

I was definitely a better mother before I had the baby.

As a child, I had certain goals imprinted deep within my heart. My first goal was to become a famous fashion designer slash part-time air hostess. My second goal was to become the first-ever Asian member of "Young Talent Time," an Australian talent television show that aired back in the '80s.

Then, of course, my third and ultimate goal was to marry a handsome man so I could have a baby and become the most amazing, nurturing mother that ever existed on the planet.

I knew what motherhood entailed. As a child, I had plenty of practice playing "Mothers and Fathers."

Sure enough, we had our episodes of panic when our Cabbage Patch Kids were crying, or when our Barbies didn't get along with the tribe. But all crisis would end once we rescued them, smothering and suffocating them in our tiny tracksuit-covered arms.

There was safety in the make-believe world of parenting because we only played out the "best bits." For some reason, I was often designated as the father in the game. Don't ask me how. Nevertheless, I decided that parenting would be a magical experience.

As a teenager, I moved on to my next phase with babies – window shopping. I'd pick out five or six of my favorite babies and toddlers that I admired at shopping centers, parties, or at church. They were the cutest, chubbiest ones, the toddlers with the sweet blue eyes or the blonde, wispy hair.

I would imagine having six children living in our picket-fenced home in the near-distant future. Surely their cute looks would guarantee fun times ahead. My very Asian boyfriend, at that time, would give me that look with one eyebrow raised.

"And how, exactly, do you plan to get a baby with blue eyes?"

However, something happened in my twenties that brought baby desires to a halt. I was introduced to the world of travel with my fiancé Sheldon – and I loved it!

We quickly postponed any wish for children. Seeing other parents struggling to cross the road with a stroller in the middle of busy Thailand and the amount of luggage they carried on board made us realize how challenging it would be to do what we enjoyed with a baby. We were having so much fun experiencing, for the first time, thrill-seeking activities in New Zealand, Thailand, and the Pacific Islands. Our idea of fun just didn't fit in the same sentence as the word, "baby."

I enjoyed the freedom of being able go where I wanted and do whatever I willed. "Let's postpone that as much as possible," I told Sheldon. "It's better being an aunty and being able to hand them back."

Plus, Sheldon and I were still "in love." That was a big deal. I actually looked forward to seeing him arrive home. We watched movies together and we thought something was wrong with us because we enjoyed each other's company. Life was perfect.

Nevertheless, the baby question kept firing back at us from all directions with full ammunition. Sheldon and I were officially married, so we were asked the grand question whichever direction we took. Forget about, "Hello."

"When are you going to have a baby?" was the greeting we would receive instantaneously upon entering a room.

Sheldon and I must have had neon signs on the tops of our heads stating, "Please ask us about having a baby," because there were times we found ourselves blankly nodding away while being lectured to by a relative on the topic. Somewhere in the backs of our minds we'd be thinking, *Didn't we start this conversation talking about barbecue recipes?*

One time, I turned up at a function as a well-intending aunty looked at me with wide eyes and exclaimed, "Congratulations!"

I looked at her apologetically, quietly replying, "Sorry. I've just been to an all-you-can-eat buffet. That's all. Just a food baby."

My parents were craving a grandchild. They even offered prize money for the first baby to pop out. Let me unravel how our Maliwat household worked. Whenever my parents felt us siblings were a little slow and needed a push, a grand money prize was set up. Fortunately, Sheldon and I won the "First to Get Married" prize and, as I write, I'm already aware of the "Have a Second Baby Foundation."

There was a bit of peer group pressure, since my parents were officially the last in the Filipino community to experience the miracle of grandchildren.

I was absolutely certain of one thing. I didn't want a baby....yet. They were much better enjoyed from afar.

Regardless of my intentions, the Universe had other plans. It gave me a big kick from behind to move things along.

I saw the sign...

It was February 10, 2008. My birthday. Sheldon traveled overseas to visit his grandparents, so it was the first time we were apart as a married couple.

We had just moved into our first home together, an apartment in the inner western suburbs of Sydney. During the painful process of house hunting throughout the year, we used the "hypothetical kid" test to work out whether the home was right for us. *Could we carry the groceries and "the kid" up all those stairs? Do we have parking so we can transfer "the kid" easily?*

This home was perfect because it had a private gated garden. Sheldon looked at me and said, "This place would be great. We could chuck 'the kid' into that garden when it needed something to do."

Fortunately, we were blessed with a great real estate agent and became the new home owners. Yeah!

I spent hours decorating the home and painting walls so it would be our designer oasis of peace. Soothing colors coordinated with our brand new rustic furniture, free from garish bright colors that would later be found on Fisher-Price toys. I ensured I had a part modernist and part Thai theme going on, and it was our couple retreat house – our place of Zen.

Back then, it was also an injury-free zone. There were no pointy fairy figurines or Lego pieces to accidently step on in the night. No texters or crayons on the floor to slip on. I swear, I could have slipped easily into Thai Chi or meditated all day.

So there I was, left alone for the first time, on my birthday. After having a small housewarming cocktail karaoke party the night before, I sat in the house, pondering what to do next.

My parents held their usual annual birthday dinner for me back at their house. It was great to feel a little less isolated. Afterwards, I made my way home.

As I drove nonchalantly along the freeway, I reflected on how I had never felt so alone without Sheldon on my birthday. I actually felt a little bit sad. My eyes gazed on the road ahead of me.

Unexpectedly, in that moment of time, I saw a shooting star. I'd only seen a few in my life. I had heard the legends that wishing on a star granted your wish. There was that anthem by Disney I never gave much attention to. I thought to myself, *When you wish upon a star...*

I don't know why, but I said to the Universe, "Please give me a baby." Then I forgot all about it.

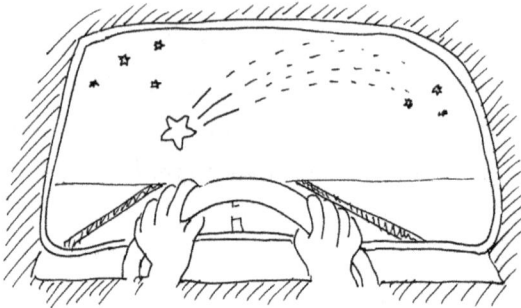

Two weeks later, when Sheldon returned, life resumed back to normal. In those days, I was teaching visual arts at a private college, but wasn't feeling very well. My work colleague and close friend Miranda asked me, "Perhaps you are pregnant?"

Could it be possible? Sheldon had been overseas so the chances were slim. The only affair I had was with Jake Gyllenhaal in my dreams.

Miranda answered, "Honey, my husband had nearly chopped his leg off a month before I fell pregnant and I wondered how that happened."

I went home and eagerly took a test that day. Following the instructions, I watched in slow motion as the positive sign became darker. I shrilled with joy! "I'm having a baby!"

"It's an immaculate conception," Sheldon blurted out.

True. Apart from Sheldon being overseas, I didn't actually recall letting him even near me in the bedroom for the past month. I liked to put up my great dividing wall of pillows right in the middle of our queen bed so I could finish that book. I put aside the mystery of how it happened and rejoiced anyway – We were having a baby!

Hmmm...

In an ecstatic bliss, I fell to my knees thanking God for everything. But that quickly turned into terror that night as I tossed and turned, realizing nine months down the track I would actually be going through labor! It didn't help that just before bedtime I did a little research on YouTube and watched horrific videos of women screeching in labor. Pleasant dreams, Anna.

Let's do a little You Tube research on giving birth.

Nevertheless, the next day I was increasingly excited. We were having a Christmas baby! In my mind, I set up the crib in the spare room and had the perfect stroller picked out as we arrived ever so calmly to social events. That same night, we visited my sister-in-law in the hospital as she had just given birth to my nephew. I quietly anticipated that I would be in the same position in nine months.

An unexpected journey...

My high soon came crashing down when everything drastically changed within eight weeks.

I was teaching, and during a break I didn't feel well. Miranda looked at me and said, "You should go to the doctor now."

I didn't listen to her advice. Instead, I decided to stick it through to the end of the day and pass by the doctor's office in the afternoon. In my last visual arts class, I even carried heavy blocks of clay.

The doctor looked at me sternly and gave me instructions. "Do not do anything or lift anything. Go home and put your feet up and just rest."

I panicked, drove home, and put my legs up. *Please, please, please baby, survive.*

By the evening, I had already miscarried. I had heard about miscarriages before, but I did not expect to feel the huge wave of pain inside like I never had before. Before then, I thought miscarriages were a minor physical loss that was easy to get over because they were so common, like getting over the flu. It was not what I expected. Now I understood what other mothers had experienced.

Despite only being eight weeks old in gestation, I had a connection with my little one and I wanted to protect him or her. I knew technically he or she was just a fetus, yet this was our baby. The hardest thing was that I had nothing physical I could embrace or hold onto to say good-bye.

I grabbed the pillow and hugged it. It was the only tangible thing I could hold onto. *How could this happen to us?*

The next day at the hospital, I couldn't stop crying. The doctor gave me the statistics of miscarriage and it was very common. Why was I so emotional? I felt like I was mourning a person's death even though my baby hadn't even been born. How could women go through this multiple times?

I must admit, the way I experienced it and handled it was extreme. I began texting people, "Please pray for my baby in heaven." Somehow asking them to pray for our baby made the baby real and validated his or her existence. Friends and family called to encourage me.

"Don't worry, Anna. There will be a next time."

"I've been through, it too."

One friend's words really stayed with me: "You deserve a very, very healthy baby. The next one will be a strong baby."

Even my hilarious past flat mate said, "Anna, I know you are dramatic. You need to vent out your emotions. If you could, you'd do a liturgical dance about this experience."

That's true. If there was any evidence of Allegra taking after me, this was my dramatic moment.

My supervisor told me to take the week off and watch mindless TV to get over it. But I still couldn't get over this. How did other mothers move on?

I researched online and read about other mothers gaining closure by naming their babies and farewelling them through planting trees or doing some commemorative ceremony.

So that's what we did. Sheldon bought a bare pink camellia tree, planted it in our garden, dedicating it to our baby. I wrote a farewell letter and we named our baby Liam.

We drove to Rodd Point, a beautiful location by the water nearby. As I read our farewell letter, Sheldon dropped flowers into the water.

It was a dark and cloudy day. Before we left, I said one last quiet prayer: *Liam, could you please send over another baby?*

The next thing that happened sounds like a melodramatic movie, but it did happen. The one thing Sheldon and I remember distinctly was how the clouds opened up after that prayer, and rays of light came shining down over the water where we had laid the flowers.

Afterwards, life felt a little empty and dark. Sheldon was so sweet. He booked a weekend trip away to Canberra to relax and rejuvenate from all the emotional drama. We also refocused on what we wanted to do in life. Perhaps we could move overseas to work?

Instead of a dramatic life change, we decided to follow one of our dreams, which was to snorkel at the Great Barrier Reef. So I booked a week away in July.

A prayer answered...

There was one thing that came out of this experience. I was determined to have another baby more than ever! It was the strongest desire I ever had in life.

The doctor told me to wait three months before trying again, but I had searched through some forums online and discovered that there was a slightly higher chance to become pregnant right after a miscarriage.

I just had one thing working against me. I had lupus. I was told by my specialist that women with this chronic autoimmune disease had a lower chance of becoming pregnant and a greater risk carrying a pregnancy to full term. There was a certain antibody produced that could kill the baby.

This could be remedied by having an injection every day through-out the pregnancy. I had the test done and, thank goodness, it was negative – but that could change in any moment. This meant we needed to try straight away!

The staff at the school where I taught was exceptional. I received tips and advice from other women who struggled to carry a pregnancy to full term.

One staff member I hardly knew came up to me and gave me a little medal of St. Gerard. She said, "Pin this to your clothes and wear it every day. Pray to St. Gerard, the patron saint of pregnancies, to intercede for you to have a baby."

I had never heard of St. Gerard, so I did some research, and found out he was the saint to pray to when women had trouble with pregnancy. I began praying for help immediately.

Within two weeks, I lost my medal. I went to the church and was relieved to find another one. The woman who gave it to me said, "I couldn't have children. After I prayed to St. Gerard, I had four kids." I wore that medal every day till the day Allegra was born.

My "Make a Baby" Recipe

So it began – my campaign to have a baby! I was like a crazy scientist finding out exactly every detail and tip I could find to mathematically increase my probability of conception. I came up with a list – mostly for my husband.

Sheldon must:

Wear loose clothing

Not drink coffee

Drink lots of water

And......

Sheldon would interrupt my rattling. "I think you forgot something. Shouldn't we be, um, having sex?"

"Yes, but that's the least of my priorities. Back to the list of things YOU need to do."

My girlfriends gave me tips. One told me that sex should not happen all the time. He needed to "save it up" for the big moment. I also researched blogs. Some theories out there were bizarre. Use egg whites for lubricant? No, thanks.

So, I barred Sheldon away from me the whole month, and then when it came to the right time according to my equation, I would yell out, "NOW!"

The whole thing would be over in five minutes, with Sheldon disorientated. "I believe I've just been raped."

Still, no pregnancy. I decided to take it to new measures. I had read good reviews about a super product that was sold in America. The theory was, it was a lubricant that helped sperm swim faster. Just like those special swim suits the Olympians wear to win gold

– except my gold would be my prize baby. I ordered it online and it arrived in the mail.

The next "Now!" moment I had, we got straight to business. Sheldon was relieved that this time it wasn't just a rape. Right in the middle of a heated moment, I abruptly stopped him and said, "Can you hold on for a moment?"

I pulled open the drawer, opened the packaging, and pulled out a contraption. I unfolded the tiny instruction booklet with microscopic writing and began reading the pragmatic instructions.

"Step one...Step two...." There was a fair bit to go through.

Sheldon looked at me. "You have got to be kidding me. Why didn't you read the instructions before?"

I hadn't thought of that. Thus was the prelude to Allegra's creation. Not quite "50 Shades of Grey."

A month later, we were invited to a friend's birthday. It was a gypsy themed party complete with a tarot card reader that she hired. I never took tarot card readings seriously, but to get into the spirit of the party, I thought it would be fun to try.

She pulled out some cards saying, "Next year by Easter you will be extremely happy. You will have a baby boy."

In fact, she could see two children in the future. I yelled over to Sheldon, who was half drunk, "Did you hear that? We'll have our baby by Easter!"

Sheldon looked at me, disoriented. "Yeah, whatever."

Well, at least the card reader got it half right.

The very next day after my great gypsy revelation, I had the strange symptoms once more, so I took the pregnancy test. Negative. Oh, well. But the next day, I kept getting the feeling that I was pregnant. Did I want this so badly that I was creating the symptoms? I took another test. Negative.

I shared my crazy "I think I'm pregnant – I think I'm not" feeling with Miranda.

She said, "Try it one more time."

There was one pregnancy test left, so I took it at home and stood in the bathroom, anxiously waiting for the result. Once again, a negative sign came up instantly.

"Oh, well. I was just imagining things." I was ready to throw it in the bin when, a couple of minutes later, something else started appearing. A faint positive could be seen. A faint positive could be seen!

"Sheldon! We're having a baby!"

Is it? Or Isn't it?

The baby's due date was February 10, 2009 – my birthday and exactly a year after I wished upon that shooting star. Once again, I was on top of the world. But this pregnancy was not without trouble. Six weeks into the pregnancy, I was having problems. The doctor told me, "Don't get too excited about the pregnancy. The ultrasound shows the placenta could detach. Just think of it this way. You are either having a baby or a miscarriage." I prepared myself for the worst.

Two weeks later, to my horror, I felt a big stab of pain. I went to get a blood test again. Up until then, my pregnancy hormone levels were quite high, which indicated I still had a normal pregnancy. I called the doctor for the results. The long silence indicated something wrong.

"Your results show that your pregnancy hormone has dropped down so low. I'm sorry. You've had another miscarriage. I suggest you go to the hospital to get yourself checked."

Second time miscarriage wasn't so bad. I wasn't traumatized like the first time. I broke the news to Sheldon. I told my family and friends and I felt all right. It was probably my lupus. I would just wait around for the miscarriage to take place and go get a check-up the next day.

Despite it all, Sheldon had faith and hope to continue praying to St. Gerard. By the morning, I received another unexpected phone call. Another doctor from the same medical center had picked up my results and demanded to see me immediately. He was abrupt.

I got there and I was surprised with his greeting,

"Your baby is dead."

I said, "I know. The other doctor told me. I'm on my way to the hospital." The other doctor was gentle and kind by comparison.

"There's no point going to the hospital. Your baby is dead and all gone." He lacked a little sensitivity. I don't know why I kept conversing with him.

"The strange thing is, I'm waiting for the big miscarriage, but it hasn't happened yet. Does that take a while?"

"It's already happened. It happened already when you went to the bathroom and you didn't notice."

I knew a miscarriage was definitely noticeable.

"Shouldn't I get an ultrasound to check?"

"Yes, but because it's not urgent I'm not going to book it for you. You can do it yourself, maybe in two weeks."

So I left and decided not to pass by the hospital. A little numb, I headed straight for sushi and began eating food that was on the banned list for pregnant women.

At least we had a holiday to look forward to. It would be hard to get an appointment for an ultrasound immediately. Thank goodness the woman on the phone booked me for an appointment that very day.

I arrived and told the lady, "I've had a miscarriage and just need to get checked for whether I need curettage."

She started the scan as I lay there, emotionless on the reclined chair. I thought, *Let's just get this over with.*

As she scanned with one hand and typed with the other, she pointed something out to me on the screen. There was tiny, fuzzy spot flashing.

"Your baby's heart is beating."

Chapter 2

The Great Barrier – Morning Sickness

"What did you just say?" The next few minutes were a whirlwind of thoughts mixed with feelings of joy and disbelief. I stood there, stunned, as I waited to collect the official report.

They gave me a print-out of the ultrasound. I could see my precious little "smudge" that had been flashing earlier on the screen. How did this happen? My pregnancy hormone level had dropped – was that test faulty?

My shock was interrupted by the ringing of my cell phone. It was my old flat mate calling to give his condolences. I exclaimed, "My baby is alive! The heart is beating... the heart is beating!"

I called Sheldon straight away and he wasn't surprised. "That's great. I knew deep inside there was still hope."

Then more calls started rolling in beginning with, "Anna I'm so sorry to hear...." abruptly changing to, "What did you just say?"

I rushed back to see the caring doctor I had seen earlier.

Bewildered, he said, "I can't explain it... how your baby is still alive. It could be a faulty hormone test. You'd better get tested again. In the meantime, just be happy!"

I got retested every day for the next four days. The original test hadn't been faulty because my subsequent results showed a very low pregnancy hormone level slowly increasing day by day. Up until now, no one has been able to medically explain it.

Looking back, it made perfect sense. Allegra would have never settled for an ordinary entrance to the world. She would want nothing less than a full-staged Broadway drama beginning with the pregnancy.

I arrived home. There at my door was a delivery of the most beautiful flowers from the staff at my school. Attached was a note: "Dear Anna, We are sorry to hear the news. Thinking of you." They were so thoughtful.

It was a strange situation, indeed. I felt like I dramatically shifted from being at a funeral to joining a huge celebration.

There were still some minor complications with the placenta causing bleeding; nevertheless, I shared my abundant news with family and friends.

"Everybody, I'm having a pregnancy or a miscarriage! Isn't that great?"

They didn't quite know how to react. "Err... congratulations?" I suppose it wasn't your standard news.

I was absolutely determined to take extreme care with this pregnancy. Some arrangements were made at work to lighten my load, and we prayed like crazy for the life of our little fighter.

There was one slight thing I had overlooked. I remembered that I had booked that adventure-packed, thrill-seeking vacation to the Great Barrier Reef in little over a month. This would get interesting.

"Are you crazy?" Well, the doctor didn't exactly say that, but I knew he was thinking it. "Cancel the trip. What happens if you have a miscarriage? You could go on this trip anytime! You could lose the baby."

That sent me into a slight panic.

I shopped around for other opinions. Another doctor told me, "Go. You will probably be more relaxed there in the warm weather, than here in the miserable cold of winter. Besides, if anything happens, there are hospitals there. Just be careful not to strain yourself."

Even friends had their opinions, from, "Take care of your pregnancy by relaxing in the sun," to "I can't believe you are putting your baby at risk!"

"Relaxing in the sun" won by a margin.

My strong man Sheldon carried the luggage and I didn't lift a finger. I sent our baby psychic messages to hang in there. Because of the lupus, I worried every single second whether this baby would survive the pregnancy.

Just before we left for the airport, Sheldon said something significant to me.

"Have a look outside our window."

I peered through our blinds and saw that a beautiful single flower had bloomed on our otherwise-barren commemorative tree we had planted for Liam.

"This must be a sign from Liam that everything is going to be okay with our baby."

I reclined in my airplane seat, melting into the imaginary brochure inside my head. Sun, tropical weather, lying at the beach. What could possibly be better?

"I'm going to vomit!"

I had read in books that morning sickness was something women experienced in the first twelve weeks of pregnancy. I was one of the fortunate ones lucky enough to have six-month, 24-hour-a-day morning sickness beginning at the Great Barrier Reef.

The pregnancy books also tell you that certain foods can make you feel sick. In my case, food, trucks, the stove top, even the movie I watched on television, "The Golden Compass," made me feel sick. Sorry, Nicole Kidman. Don't take my desire to puke personally.

After trying every anti-vomit solution there was, Sheldon took me to the chemist in Port Douglas to buy anti-vomit pills.

"Just looking at the anti-vomit pills make me want to vomit!"

Forget fancy restaurants and sightseeing; our two-week adventure involved staying within a 30-second dash to the nearest toilet.

"Does Seafolly make you feel sick?" Sheldon asked. Earlier that week, I had spotted a Seafolly swimwear sale in Cairns. For an entire 30 minutes, my nausea halted as I shopped for bargains.

"No." Swimwear fit in a special anti-vomit category, and I wouldn't be surprised if this had something to do with Allegra's love for bikinis.

Despite the nausea, I was still determined to see all those cute little damn fishes we traveled to see. We went ahead with the two snorkelling trips to the Great Barrier Reef and a Daintree National Park day tour.

What in the world was I thinking? I sat on the bumpy boat, looking around me.

It was mostly young, fit backpackers in their twenties, and there I was, constantly holding a bag to my face. Morning sickness and sea sickness? What a combination! If you haven't tried it, here's one word of advice... don't!

To add icing to the cake, the roundtrip to the reef was three hours long and the forecast was extra choppy waters.

After one and a half hours, we finally made it to our snorkeling destination and the boat stopped. I assessed the situation. It didn't look quite like my brochure. It was an overcast day and the waters were rough. The thrill seekers, along with Sheldon, excitedly jumped in the water.

"Woo hoo!"

Everyone was in the water, except the puking mother-to-be.

What a predicament. *Should I jump into the choppy water or stay on the rocking boat that added seasickness to my morning sickness?* I chose the choppy water.

For a brief moment, I saw the coral under the sea, but poor visibility and the strong current got me worrying. *Anna, please do not have a Great Barrier miscarriage at sea – especially on Nemo!* After five minutes, I thought it was too risky and sat back on the boat, while Sheldon had the time of his life.

Did I see fish that day? Not really. Did I witness the loving kindness of mankind? Yes. On the trip back, sitting permanently fixed with a bag to my mouth, empathetic backpackers took turns kindly donating their vomit bags to me.

Our second trip out to the reef was far more magical than the first. It was a fancier company with a larger, sophisticated boat and better croissants. The weather was glorious.

I still had to bear with the three-hour round trip, but thanks to my loving husband, who was willing to be drenched with the ocean, we sat outside the boat where fresh air and focusing on the horizon kept me from being sick.

We arrived at our spot and I almost broke into a little mermaid dance. We were surrounded by beautiful aqua water in the middle of the reef, with baby sharks swimming close to the edge of the boat. Now this was the real Great Barrier Reef.

I learned my lesson from the last trip, and firmly decided to stay on the boat. When the crowds cleared, one of the instructors asked me, "Why aren't you going in?"

"I just can't swim right now," I answered.

"Oh, you don't know how to swim. That's all right. I will tie you to a flotation device and pull you with a rope. I'll swim ahead of you. You can't come all this way and NOT see the coral."

He did have a point. I didn't mind that he thought I technically couldn't swim. That was a better excuse than possible miscarriage at sea.

I took up his offer and I'm glad that I did. He dragged me along the ocean like I was a five-year-old being pulled by my daddy – except he happened to be young, fit, tanned, and with abs. It was amazing – I meant the fish. We headed back to our hotel and I was grateful for the experience. Our baby had officially visited a wonder of the world and experienced the wonder of "Baywatch" bodies.

What else did we see on the rest of that holiday? Sheldon saw crocodiles, waterfalls, and beautiful nature while I pretty much saw my feet from crouching over. At least I wore my best shoes.

Overall, the best part of our tropical Queensland adventure was that our little baby survived.

Chapter 3

Parenthood Fantasies

This was one of the rare moments in my life when I was proud to develop a meaningful belly. Meaningful because it wasn't just filled with food and fat. My little person was in there – probably using my padding as a trampoline.

I had survived the first trimester and absolutely refused to get my hopes up by purchasing any baby items. Anything could happen from a lupus point of view, so I didn't want to get too excited.

When I finally reached 23 weeks of pregnancy, I turned to Sheldon and said, "I think we are actually having this baby."

One memorable day, I decided to collect scans from the medical centre. That was when I encountered that crazy doctor again. He looked at me and insisted I step into the room.

After closing the door, he pulled out the report and stuck the ultrasound images on his light box.

"This baby should be dead."

He was so tactful. Obviously, he had seen my tummy growing and wondered why I was still pregnant. For some reason, I stayed in the room, so he went on with his verdict.

"If it is alive, it is deformed."

Everything he had said so far didn't make sense. "But the report says the baby is alive and growing healthy?"

With absolute certainty he declared, "I don't read those reports. I interpret the results myself."

I had read about pregnancies in which the fetus was not a fetus, but actually deformed cells appearing to be healthy. These deformed cells could be dangerous and cancerous if left to grow.

Anxious, I imagined the worst possible situation, *Oh my goodness, what if this baby is actually cancerous cells that are going to kill me?* It turned into a movie in my head. I rushed over to my neighbor and knocked on the door. I didn't know where to turn.

Maria and John were Italian. I could usually hear their passionate arguments, including colorful language, across the hallway. Maria opened the door and I exclaimed, "The doctor says the baby is deformed."

She calmed me down and, with passionate certainty, told me, "Believe me. Your baby is going to be just fine. Your baby is a fighter."

I realized that returning to the psycho doctor and having heart attack every time I encountered him was not helping me. As I sat on Maria's couch, her daughter suggested I swap hospitals for an excellent hospital in another location.

Due to the high-risk nature of my pregnancy with having lupus, I was able to transfer hospitals. My lupus specialist recommended me to the care of a fantastic obstetrician I could trust.

I arrived at the new hospital for my first check-up. It was a beautiful hospital for women, with hardly any waiting and very helpful staff. I had heard excellent reviews from friends who had babies there.

My obstetrician checked everything and reassured me. "Your baby is completely healthy and growing as expected."

The obstetrician did raise one issue. "My main concern regarding the lupus is not the pregnancy. My real concern is post-partum. With lupus, you need to make sure you have someone to help you."

I hadn't thought about caring for a baby with lupus. I knew I had to be careful not to get too stressed and make sure I was well rested to prevent a flare-up. How hard would it be? We decided to live with my in-laws for three weeks after the birth, for preventive measures. In reality, this ended up stretching to five whole months.

Sheldon and I continued to pray every night for our little fighter. Before leaving for work, Sheldon would kiss my tummy goodbye. At first it was, "Bye, zygote," and eventually the cells moved up in ranking and were addressed as, "Bye, baby."

This was around the time I began having my three-fold parenthood fantasies.

My first fantasy: Life would be perfect with a baby

I had seen those Pumpkin Patch catalogues featuring babies with perfect dimples and wide eyes shining. I enjoyed those Huggies television commercials with laughing babies completely sanitized in a poop and vomit-free environment.

I must admit, I may have been selective with what I chose to see, but there were other sources that contributed to my first fantasy.

After all, didn't Rachel on "Friends" look fantastic after giving birth to her little Emma? After her birth, baby Emma magically disappeared with a convenient baby sitter while Rachel looked fabulous working in the fashion industry.

Then there was that show, "Full House," in which Lori Loughlin looked stunning with her Cindy Crawford hairstyle as she sat on the couch and her twin toddlers laughed around her.

I had my "real" sources, as well. Countless celebrities looked great after popping out babies. They were always pictured frolicking somewhere like the French Riviera soon after. It may have slipped my mind that celebrities had plenty of money to hire nannies, trainers, cooks, cleaners, and a Hollywood hair stylist named Ken Paves.

Deducing from my superficial sources, life would be picture-perfect once our baby was born. If Heidi Klum could be a glamazon after four kids, I could do it with one. Hence, this was the mother movie I played in my mind:

I would have my "magic moment" labor. Baby would be fitted in its cute Pumpkin Patch outfit and come home from the hospital. Baby would simply sleep most of the day and wake up giggling.

I would be a patient, loving, organic, stay-at-home mom relishing every second with my baby. Sheldon would come home at a convenient time with patience and love. We would tuck baby in bed and, just like Tom Cruise, say to our baby, "You complete me." Sheldon and I would finish with quality bonding time together being in love.

In reality, years later "bonding time" became one hour crashed out on the couch watching "Ladette to Lady," If we were lucky.

As soon-to-be parents, we were clueless. I do recall my best friend saying, "Labor is not the hard bit. Wait until you have to take care of the baby. Sleep deprivation is worse than labor pains. It'll kill you."

That message flowed in one ear and out the other. No room for that message. My thoughts were firmly fixed on the pretty crib, the matching drapes, and the lovely little diaper stacker.

I read all the books regarding every little aspect of pregnancy, but hardly any reading material on what to expect once the baby came out. We received books that guaranteed full-proof methods for sleep settling. We would keep them on the shelf just in case there were any hiccups.

My second fantasy: Our baby would be quiet, meek, and gentle

Sheldon and I also had a fantasy about the personality of our baby. Since Sheldon was gentle, calm, patient, and wise, I vividly pictured our child having the same demeanour and personality traits.

He rarely raised his voice and never acted irrationally. I was a little more flamboyant and creative. However, growing up together we were shy, quiet, and hardworking.

I hardly spoke in my first years of schooling, so much so that my second grade teacher sarcastically whispered my name when it came to roll call. I would respond by saying, "I can't hear you," and she'd say, "I can't either."

Sheldon's school reports revealed the same. He rarely spoke out at school. In fact, I'm pretty sure we had the same comments written about us in reports: A diligent and conscientious student. That meant we were so quiet that we saved the teachers a headache. Just doing the calculations in my head, our child would surely inherit the same calm and quiet genes.

In reality, from the moment Allegra entered the earth she was the complete opposite.

Years later, I was asked the question by day care teachers, "Were you and your husband loud or, let's say, dramatic when you were younger? Allegra is the loudest, dramatic, confident child in the entire day care."

Better yet, "Anna, were you on something when you were pregnant? Because when all the children have finished playing and are exhausted, Allegra looks like the party is just beginning."

No, I wasn't doing drugs in pregnancy. What kind of mother did she think I was? Although it did cross my mind after the baby came out.

My third fantasy: We couldn't wait to meet our son

When most people are asked the question, "Do you prefer a boy or a girl?" they respond with the most loving answer. "We don't mind just as long as our baby is healthy."

In our case, Sheldon and I were very specific. "We want a boy."

Our "boy fantasy" began with that gypsy party, the day before I found out I was pregnant. Blame it on the tarot card reader. She told me, "You are having a boy by Easter and you will experience happiness beyond belief." We were thrilled!

Later, Sheldon shared his theory. "You know Allegra did look like a boy when she was born. Perhaps the tarot card reader saw into the future and, you know, mistook her for a boy."

Then there was the Filipino necklace test that determined the sex of the baby. Apparently, holding a necklace between your fingers and watching whether it swung side to side or round and round determined whether you were having a girl or a boy.

I still remember the defining moment when my friend dangled the necklace. She looked up, fixing her eyes on mine. "The necklace has spoken. It's a boy!" We took two of these trustworthy tests.

There were other reasons for wanting a boy. I surveyed my colleagues at school. "Which is easier to raise?"

"Have a boy, Anna. Boys are so wonderful and easy and simple. They love their moms and want to stay home with you forever, if they could. Girls are drama. They argue about the Lisa Ho dress that I just paid $300 for, which they can't wear again to another formal."

I understood quickly. I didn't want formal dress drama. I never caused formal dress drama growing up, as I remember sewing my own dresses. But, I still didn't want the mother-daughter arguments, fueled with hormonal mood swings, building up to a great diva tragedy.

I refused to have a princess. While I loved my students overall, teaching at an all girl's school, I was a little bit over the drama associated with girls. I had memories of turning up to a class asking, "Where is half of my year eight class?"

"Mrs Garcia, they are in the restroom comforting a girl who is crying. She broke up with her boyfriend."

So our vision was set in stone. We were going to have a meek boy, as though we had ordered him online. I clicked the boy with the soccer outfit.

The ultrasound revealed

The day we had our second trimester ultrasound was exciting. Sheldon finally had a day off work, so it was our first appointment together. They began showing us images of the baby's organs. We were grateful everything looked healthy.

Finally she asked, "Would you like to know the sex of your baby?" Confirming our child's male sex would be great. We were excited.

After a little bit of waiting, she finally said, "Congratulations! You are having a girl."

We couldn't speak for two hours. Already, images of diva tantrums were brewing in our minds while driving home.

We certainly didn't want a "Ja'Mie." Ja'Mie King was a hilarious, spoiled character from a funny Australian television series, "Summer Heights High."

She was an over-achieving, jealous, bitchy girl who caused drama and put others down. In particular, she had disrespectful, screaming fights with her mother, who just bore it all. We found her funny, but would have absolutely dreaded having a diva daughter like her.

Sitting in the car, Sheldon finally broke the silence with a famous line from Ja'Mie King. "You're such an f@#$%* b*@%#, Mom!"

No! I screamed silently within. What if she was a diva? A drama queen?

"Oh, no," I whispered.

A couple of weeks down the track, we had calmed ourselves down. It might not be so bad; she may not be a drama queen. We held our hopes high.

Sheldon started having other ideas. "I hope our daughter is only medium-pretty. I don't want her to get by in life by her looks. I want her to fight through life." He was so passionate about this, scrunching his fist and waving it through the air as he spoke. It was like he was giving a speech for the Nobel Peace Prize.

Later, I asked him, "Did you get what you wanted?"

He answered, "Um, yep." He deduced this from the comments we received on Facebook. While other parents' kids got into modeling, or received comments like, "She's so pretty," we always got, "She's hilarious," "She's so interesting," and even, "She's so strange." Don't worry. We do believe our daughter is beautiful.

She'll never get a job with that name...

I started the name-searching process. We had the same problem that couples all over the world have. We couldn't agree on a name.

Having had a fairly ordinary name – so ordinary it could be spelled backwards and still be the same – I wanted a unique, international name. Sheldon, having a more unique name, wanted an ordinary, popular name.

I searched relentlessly online. "What about Latonya, Reshaunda, or Safiya?"

"No. She will never get a job with those names."

So this was our criteria: we needed a name that was interesting, but enabled her to apply for a job.

I recalled watching a funny movie called "Hitch," which featured a glamorous character named Allegra, played by the supermodel Amber Valetta.

I loved that name. It had edge, it had glamour, and Will Smith wasn't bad. I researched the meaning online: "Lively and cheery." I was happy with that, plus there was a link to high fashion. I found out that Versace's granddaughter was named Allegra Versace.

Surprisingly, Sheldon also approved. Together, we decided she would be named Allegra Marcheline Garcia.

Three years later, Allegra took the liberty to change her own name. When my sister Maria asked, "What's your name?" Allegra pronounced, "Allegra M. Garcia."

"What does the 'M' stand for?"

"McDonald's."

Sheldon and Anna Garcia's heiress eventually became known as Allegra McDonald's Garcia.

Last-minute advice...

Time was moving quickly and I couldn't believe our baby had made it to the final trimester. I was weeks from giving birth and absolutely thrilled.

My sister organized my baby shower. As we ate cupcakes and delicious desserts, I gathered all the last tips and advice from my friends who had been through it all before.

One friend had visualized a serene, pain-free birth, and was fortunate enough to have only mild pains and a quick labor. I made a mental note: *Begin visualizing a Zen birth immediately.*

Another friend recommended a TENS machine. It was a device which you would attach to your back that pulsated and distracted you from your contractions. She used it, didn't need any drugs, and said her contractions were so mild. Second mental note: *Book the TENS machine.*

I heard yoga and swimming were good, so I did plenty of that. I was so prepared. Everything would lead to a perfect birth.

One mother's experience really stuck with me. "I had pain in my labor, but Anna, it is so worth it. My daughter is my biggest achievement in my life. This is what I am most proud of."

Wow. I couldn't wait for my turn. With the baby's room all set up and a bassinette ready at my in-laws' house, we were ready to go.

Prenatal Class

Our final preparation was the prenatal class. We arrived at a community center and met other women who looked like they were about to burst.

Our instructor was a vibrant lady named Sarah. We sat there, amazed as she explained every little detail of what occurs in the uterus through her one-woman dramatic performance. We watched Sarah climb under a table, lay on the floor, curl up into a fetal position, and then finally be born. I almost clapped at the end. She should have won an Oscar.

She broke the myth that all babies were born cute and even confessed, "My babies looked like aliens. You can tell your babies look like aliens when visiting guests are silent, try their hardest to smile, and say 'Congratulations' instead of 'Your baby is so cute.'"

Sarah warned us, "Don't be surprised if you don't get the birthing experience that you wanted. Some women get traumatized by this instead of realizing they have a beautiful child."

What could she possibly mean? Sheldon and I couldn't understand. How could you get traumatized when a miracle had just taken place?

We finished the session with documentaries of women giving birth. As they groaned and screamed, we all questioned whether there was a way of turning back.

One man raised his hand. "I believe the gas should be available for the men."

After the emotional process, seeing a new life enter the world made every person in the room teary. It was so beautiful. The people in the video were crying. Sheldon and I were emotional.

All my life, I had seen movies depicting the entry of a child into the world as the most miraculous moment of one's life. Through such moments in movies, friendships and family feuds were mended and healed by the sight of the sleeping newborn baby.

I also heard stories from mothers about how the moment their baby came out, they forgot their pain, and the joy in their hearts was indescribable.

Sheldon and I looked forward to our own magic moment. We looked at each other with teary eyes.

"If this is how we feel just watching a video of some stranger's birth, how much more miraculous and joyful it would be when Allegra is born."

Chapter 4

The Descent of Spider-bubs

"Sheldon, it's time. I think this is it."

It was three o'clock in the morning when I started feeling the pain growing regularly. My heart was jumping in anticipation – soon we would meet our precious miracle baby.

Sheldon didn't share my enthusiasm. "Go back to bed... just false contractions... baby is coming next week," and he rolled over.

Allegra was due the following week on my birthday. However, after Sheldon pointed out if Allegra were to be born on my birthday, I'd never celebrate my birthday again, I sent out a request to the Universe to do an express service.

Perhaps Sheldon was right. Maybe it was false contractions. I went back to bed, tossing and turning as the pain became stronger.

"Sheldon, I think I am really in labor"

"Go back to bed, Anna... false labor.... baby is due next week."

There I was, in the early hours of the morning in labor, with a husband of little faith. I got up and sat in the living room, timing the contractions. They were fifteen minutes apart. I excitedly pulled out my TENS machine.

"Sheldon, really. I am in labor. The baby is coming."

All I could hear was snoring. So I lay back in bed, tossing and turning. By the morning, I put forth my labor case one more time.

"Don't worry. You are not having a baby!" Sheldon was adamant.

So I did what other women that weren't in labor did. "Let's go to that party!" It wasn't just any party. It was a party far away in the opposite direction of the hospital.

Not only that, we also packed our clothes to sleep over at my in-laws' house. "We might as well watch a DVD at our parents' house." That was also in the opposite direction of the hospital.

Do you know what it feels like mingling with guests at a barbecue in labor? I sat on a chair, quietly clenching every fifteen minutes.

"Are you ok?" my sister-in-law asked.

"Yep... I'm good... ouch.... I'm good. Mmmm... Great barbecue chicken." I could still manage to mingle.

All the aunties gave their two cents worth. "Yeah, Anna, you're having the baby soon," as they munched on their corn chips.

We retreated back to my in-laws' house, watched a DVD, and then the pain turned to excruciating. At first, I thought it was the bad acting, but finally I said, "We've got to go to the hospital now!" Finally, Sheldon believed the labor was on. We left swiftly in the night and gave our parents a heart attack in the morning when they discovered that we had mysteriously disappeared.

It had been twenty-four hours since the contractions first began. Sheldon hooked up the TENS machine. It had sticky patches that he placed on my back, connected to wires. It was like we were planting a bomb in "Mission Impossible." Every time I had a contraction, I pressed a button that detonated pulses down my back.

Did it help? I'm not really sure. It felt like little electric shocks. The type your brother gives you after rubbing his feet on the carpet. Brilliant. Double pain, contractions, and electric shocks. I guess the idea was to shoot such pain that contractions didn't seem so bad.

That was another thing. No one had ever described the feeling of contractions to me. Some women were lucky enough to experience mild cramps. My own experience was, shall I say, a thousand knives stabbing me a hundred times!

We arrived at the hospital and the nurse confirmed I was three centimetres dilated. Woo hoo! I had officially started the dilation journey. Since I had a long way to go, she suggested I go home, take some sleeping tablets, and get some rest.

Rest was a little challenging with the thousand knives stabbing in the background, but I tried my best. My mother-in-law was ringing Sheldon in panic, "Check on Anna. What if the baby comes out while she's sleeping?" If only I were that lucky.

Dilating in reverse?

By the end of the second day, we were back at the hospital. The nurse set up a bed for Sheldon, though neither of us rested that night.

The contractions transformed into absolutely intense rolling waves of pain without a break. *Aaaarrhhh...* Where was my Zen birth?

"These big contractions are good," the nurse reassured me. "They will help you dilate." But after checking me, she changed her mind. "Hmmm. You're only two centimeters dilated. Honey, you are dilating in reverse."

Dilating in reverse? Two sleepless nights and all I had was two centimeters? Did Allegra change her mind and decide to close shop? How would I make it to the end? There was only one option left.

"Give me an epidural!"

I had held off for so long because I wanted to be a drug-free hero, plus there was the Filipino taboo.

There was hesitation in her voice. "Your platelet count is too low. You will have to wait and see if you are allowed to have the epidural."

I have had two near-heart attacks in my life. Telling me I possibly couldn't have an epidural was one of them.

Thank goodness the anesthesiologist approved it and I lived. The needle was my best friend, and soon the waves of pain dulled down.

After assessing me, the doctor said, "Your baby is stuck. Your baby's head is too big."

I knew big heads ran in my family. My sister often called me Olive Oyl from the "Popeye" series because of my skinny frame and round head, kind of like a match stick. Sheldon also had a big head, so that was a double dosage. Since I looked quite small in my pregnancy, I presumed Allegra was tiny.

"Your baby is also getting distressed. You have two options. We can prick the baby's head to take a sample of blood and do some tests, or you can have an emergency Caesarean section."

After three sleepless days and feeling delirious, I said, "Get the baby out!"

They wheeled me into a cold room and all I wanted was a nice nap. Since they were doing all the work, I thought closing my eyes just for one moment couldn't possibly hurt the baby. There I was, transported relaxing on a day bed under a cabana by the beach.

A voice within woke me up. *Anna, don't fall asleep! You must be awake when Allegra comes out! Hold on for the magic moment.*

It was a battle between the cabana and the most defining moment of my life. This wasn't exactly the scenario I had expected. I lay there, drifting in and out of delirium as a partition was set up between the doctor and me. I was an observer, a third party, oblivious to the commotion in the room.

Then something shook me, literally. It wasn't the doctor. I started shaking uncontrollably from the epidural. Sheldon thought he'd be extra helpful by massaging my head so that my body and my head were shaking.

That gave me a headache. I mustered my strength and slurred out, "Stop. Don't do that." He interpreted this as, "Massage harder." Husbands are so handy.

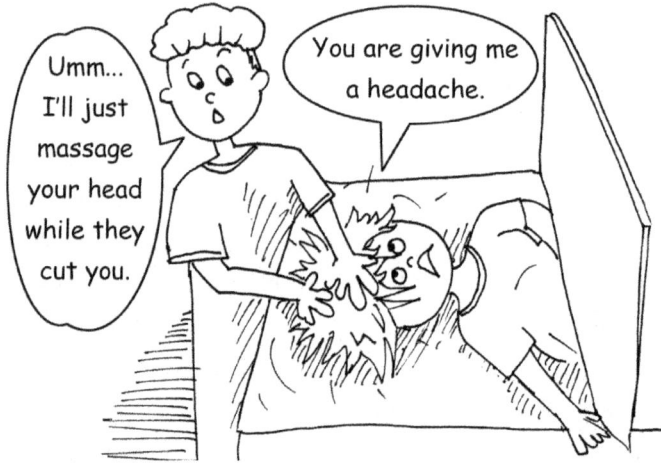

They pushed my tummy around on the other side of the sheet while I blissfully slept for another micro-second. Finally, after some fiddling on the other side, I could hear a baby crying.

Sheldon and I looked up. This was the moment.

Allegra's entry

I could only describe it as a big baby descending with arms and legs outstretched like Spider-Man and eyes wide open.

She was extremely alert, checking out the situation. Sheldon and I were in shock. For some reason, we were expecting a delicate little curled-up baby, but this one looked strong enough to punch us.

Allegra Marcheline Garcia was born at 6:20 a.m. on Monday, 2nd February 2009, at 52 centimeters long, and weighing seven pounds. It was a three-day labor.

The nurses cleaned her, wrapped her up, and handed her to us. She wasn't crying. She just intensely stared at us like she was assessing our parenting capabilities, or threatening us if we didn't do a good job. "Smile," the nurse said as she snapped our first family photo.

We were still in shock. I thought I'd be crying when Allegra arrived, but I so badly wanted to go to bed.

To be completely honest, her entrance into the world was like a delivery by Australia Post. I had been building up to this moment for the last nine months. I was waiting for that magic moment. Where was that magic moment?

It made me question, did every woman get a magic moment? Perhaps it only happened to a number of women and the rest just never spoke about it.

Perhaps it was just me, over-exhausted and delirious. I turned to Sheldon and asked him what it was like for him.

"It was like someone delivered a cappuccino."

He hadn't experienced a miraculous father moment either. What was wrong with us? Did we have hearts of stone? We felt more by watching strangers deliver on video footage than our own miracle child.

At that time, I had never heard of any mother or father who wasn't moved by the birth of their own baby. I thought we were strange. It didn't add up in my head. A miracle pregnancy and healthy baby should have produced a magic moment. It wasn't until months later when I would meet amazing, loving mothers who also did not experience a magic moment, or did not connect immediately. Love took time to grow.

They wheeled her away and told Sheldon to follow, while they stitched me up. I thought, *It doesn't matter, she is healthy, and I'm just tired. Once I have enough sleep, I'll fall in love with her.*

"Wow," the doctor said as she stitched me up. "Next time you give birth, you will need a Caesarean. Your uterus is all worn out from those contractions." I felt some stinging as she continued to stitch me up, so I told the anesthesiologist. She apologized. "Oops, better top you up with anesthesia."

I was numb from my waist down when they wheeled me away. I thought, *Finally! I can sleep.*

Little did I know that I would wait thirteen months to finally get that sleep I longed for in the hospital.

Chapter 5

Reality

Let me tell you something about sleep. It's a gift, a blessing, a treasure to savor. You'll never fully appreciate the value of the Zzzzz's until a baby decides to have a little fun with your sleep pattern. I thought my friends were kidding when they told me they hadn't slept since 2005.

I do believe my first year with Allegra was a constant state of never being fully awake and never being fully asleep. In my delirious condition with my matching dishevelled hairdo, I must have been hot stuff to my husband.

After giving birth, they wheeled me into a room. *Finally I can get some rest and respite.* Instead, I was faced with a crib containing a baby and a very confused husband.

Allegra lay there, eating her fist like a Pac-Man. She was hungry. What were we supposed to do?

The nurse picked her up and said, "You need to feed her."

How silly of me to think I had time for sleep. I had to learn the ropes of motherhood!

Though her entrance seemed uneventful compared to our vision, there was nothing ordinary about the epic journey we were about to embark upon with Allegra Marcheline Garcia.

Allegra - the perfect baby

The first hours of Allegra's life seemed to be 100% perfect. Sleeping soundly – tick. Looking like a cutie-patootie – tick. Breastfeeding not as hard as I thought – tick. I had it all figured out. All snuggled up, Allegra slept like a baby from an Anne Geddes calendar. *Awww, she was pretty cute.*

I placed her back in her crib, ready to close my eyes when…

"Surprise!" In popped my family with huge balloons and flowers. As Allegra was born early that morning, by the time I finished feeding her it was visiting hours.

"She looks like you!"

"She's long."

"She's black."

"She's white."

All the family comments started flying out.

"She looks so cute! Oh… shame about the Maliwat nose."

Fantastic. She was officially not an alien, but she inherited the Filipino flat nose. They were extremely excited about the first Maliwat grandchild. Within seconds of her entry into the world, my father had broadcast the news to the entire Filipino community. Even the neighbor's dogs knew about her.

When they finally left, I couldn't sleep. Allegra looked so blissful in her crib and she had not cried at all. *Wow*, I thought, *I'm blessed with a really good baby.* She didn't scream like the others. If there was a best baby pageant, she was clearly one of the finalists.

So instead of catching up on much-needed rest, I just stared at her in amazement. Falling in love with this baby would be easy.

At this point, I'd like to share one bit of advice: Pay attention to what you are taught in prenatal class. Sarah warned us to catch up on sleep during the initial sleeping phase. This was because, shortly after being born, babies enter a long sleeping phase to recover. We had to build up our strength for the feeding frenzy that would soon follow.

I was so clever that I threw that bit of advice out the window and chose to gaze lovingly at my perfect baby. If only I had paid attention, my week may have turned out differently.

Sheldon held Allegra one last time, stepping into fatherhood easily. He finally said his goodbyes as visiting hours wrapped up for the evening.

"Are you going to be okay?"

"Sure, how hard could it be?"

I took my medication to dull the pain from the Caesarean. After nearly four days without sleep, I was ready to transition into a deep, relaxing sleep.

"WAAAAHHHHH... WAAAAAAAHHHH... WAAAAAAHHHHH!"

The Scream

It began. I called it The Scream. This would continue to grow in amplitude and strength throughout her existence.

'WAAAAAHHH!' translated in the English dictionary means, "Drop everything and feed me now," or, "Don't you even dare think of lying me down. I need to be carried twenty-four seven."

I kept my cool. She was hungry. *No worries,* I thought. So I picked her up and began feeding her. After an hour and a half, I placed her down. "There you go, sweetie. Now go to sleep."

I crept over silently to my bed and, within two seconds, she began again.

"WAAAAAAAAH... WAAAAAAAAAAAHHH... WAAAAAAHHH"

I picked her up and repeated the same process. "There, there... poor hungry baby."

Once settled, I put her down again.

"WAAAAAAAA... WAAAAAAAAAAAAA..."

After at least four hours of the same process, I started questioning, *Is this ever going to end?*

The Feeding Frenzy

Allegra was not just hungry. She was craving-for-a-big-fat-meal hungry. I was taught in breastfeeding class that the small amount a baby received would be just the right amount since its stomach was the size of a marble. We were supposed to be biologically compatible. Allegra's stomach was the size of a soccer ball. Forget a-la-carte; she wanted the whole degustation menu.

"Keep feeding her. You are doing a good job," the nurse encouraged me. "This is what you need to go through in the first week to get your milk supply."

The first week? I hadn't even made it through the first day.

That was another aspect of breastfeeding I soon learned about. You had to keep at it non-stop for about a week to make your body supply the milk. While in the beginning, it wasn't too bad, by the end of the week it was excruciating torture. I won't even begin with the metaphors. Let's just say I envied Sheldon at one point simply because he was breastless.

So there I was on my first night, struggling to stay open like a 7-Eleven. Perhaps I could just close my eyes as I fed?

I lightly closed my eyes and I fed her through the night. After jolting a couple of times and nearly dropping her on the floor, I thought, *This certainly is not an option!*

Perhaps I could sleep with her next to me in the bed? This was something the hospital didn't recommend. I inched my way onto the bed, holding her, moving ever so slowly as my stitches caused me extreme pain.

I lay feeding her when my hallucinations began and I couldn't tell what was real and what wasn't. In my state of hallucination, I almost physically punched Allegra. I forced myself awake. *Punching the baby is also not an option.*

It was two in the morning when I realized I was in the most uncomfortable situation in my life. I could hardly move because of the Caesarean. I was in excruciating pain, with a screaming baby, and deliriously sleep-deprived for the past four days.

Please sleep, baby...please sleep....

Did they ever play this part in the movies? No. The scene always cut off at the point when everyone was happy at the hospital and passing the baby around. The next scene would be in the baby's room back at home. What about the scenes in-between? What about the feeding frenzy?

I recalled my friends sharing their experiences with me. "Don't worry, Anna. Newborns sleep all the time."

Sleep all the time? Allegra did not come from sleep-all-the-time land.

I tiptoed across to the crib, put her down again, and slowly walked away.

"WAAAAAAAAAAHHHH!"

Help!

Desperate, I called the nurse. "Help me. My baby won't stop screaming!" What I really wanted to say was, "Can you tuck this baby away, preferably somewhere soundproof?"

Salvation arrived when a nurse wrapped her up and placed her back in the hospital crib. "It's all in the wrapping." As a new parent, you also learn to origami-wrap your baby in a hundred different ways.

Allegra was quiet for two entire minutes. She must have approved of this fold. The nurse walked out the door and...

"WAAAAAAAAAAHHHH!!!!!"

There must have been a wrinkle.

I tried settling her again and again. Nothing was working. I found myself negotiating with the one-day-old bubs. "Now, Allegra, all I need is one night. Is that too much to ask?"

I was drowning in my first day of motherhood, caught in a baby rip that was dragging me out to the sea. I could see the life guards in the distance giving me the thumbs up. "Just keep feeding!"

They had this policy at the hospital - there was no saving mothers from their babies. Their belief was, you created them, and you take care of them. It was supposed to be the best way to connect with your child. So I managed to barely stay afloat through the night connecting with Allegra.

The next day, I called for reinforcement. "Sheldon, get over here straight away after work!"

There was a reason Sheldon was missing that week. Just before Allegra was born, he decided to change jobs. This meant he had no official leave. He offered to take some time off, but since he was under probation, I insisted that he didn't. It was a wise decision, as later he would be one out of three employees that survived the probationary period.

It just meant my challenging time turned into a tougher one. Sheldon could only arrive close to closing time during those five days in the hospital, so I had 30 precious minutes when he could relieve me from Allegra. I was on my own most of the time unless a visitor arrived.

It was now three days since her birth and I still hadn't showered. I was desperate, but alone with a hysterical baby. As a first-time mother, I didn't know how to just let her cry.

Fortunately, one of the guests who arrived for another lady empathized. "Why don't you shower while I hold her?"

Here's another lesson in parenting. All the simple basics like having a shower and eating become squashed into whatever little crevice you can find between feeding, settling, and cleaning the baby. Suddenly such staples for an adult become absolutely divine luxuries.

I stood in the luxury of my five-minute express shower. It wasn't quite a day spa experience with Allegra roaring outside the door. I tensed up. Now the lady sounded like she was the one needing saving, so I hurried out the door. "I'm coming. I'll save you!"

How long could a baby scream? Allegra screamed into her second day, third day, fourth day, and fifth day at the hospital. The different nurses tried various strategies such as propping up the bed at an angle and lying her on her side, but she kept crying.

On my fourth night, at three in the morning, a kind nurse, a Good Samaritan said to me, "Go get some sleep. I will walk her around the hospital."

As I lay in bed, all I could hear was Allegra screeching her lungs out like an ambulance siren getting closer and farther away as the nurse pushed her around the corridors. But even the Good Samaritan couldn't work miracles. She brought her back in.

"Sorry. She doesn't want to sleep. You should try feeding her again."

The baby warranty

Motherhood was not enjoyable at all. I couldn't eat. I couldn't sleep. I was fumbling with diapers while Allegra had green poop shooting out on the bedding. I could shower only because a stranger offered to help. Thank goodness my mother arrived. It was over an hour drive each way, but she gave me relief just for a moment so I could get my lunch.

My mother pushed the crib fearlessly, whether Allegra screamed or not. As a veteran, she shone her "Do you want to mess with me?" aura over Allegra. Yet even a veteran succumbs to embarrassment. As we attended the bathing class together, we could feel ourselves shrinking as Allegra was the only baby in the room wailing her lungs out.

I sat there on the bed by the fourth night and started to break down and cry. "I don't like this job... sob... sob." Surely I could exchange her? She was new and still under warranty.

The nurse replied, "Baby blues? It's very common with women because of lack of sleep and your hormones are all over the place."

Another kind nurse stayed up with me all night. "She's just a very hungry baby and your milk hasn't come in yet. Once your milk comes in on the fifth day, she'll be a completely different baby."

I held onto that precious figure, "five days old," when I would receive my completely different baby. In the meantime, the nurse took a little cup of formula and allowed Allegra to dip her tongue in it like a kitten. She finally slept for an hour.

My challenging time was obvious. If there was a motherhood exam, I had certainly failed module one. Like a struggling student, I watched other mothers not only pass, but receive gold stars. One mother next to me fed her baby while she was on the phone conducting a business meeting.

Wow, she's smooth, and if I'm not mistaken, her hair looks blow-waved.

On my fifth night, a nurse approached me. "I think you should stay one night longer. I'm worried you won't survive with this baby on your own."

All I wanted was to go home where I had help from the family and could sleep. She finally approved, provided I had assistance.

A ray of hope...

On my sixth day, the miraculous occurred. My milk finally arrived. Hallelujah! For the very first time that week, Allegra was content and her soccer ball tummy was full. She finally went to sleep for an entire two hours, the most she had ever slept apart from her first day.

Sheldon arrived and I was so happy to see him. I could almost see beams of light shining around him, and a sparkle reflect from his teeth. "You're here!"

I survived the ordeal. I could honestly say that the week Allegra was born was the most challenging week of my life. I could have been featured on the series "I Shouldn't Be Alive" or "Man Versus Wild."

He looked over to the cutest little baby curled up sleeping. Babies have a way of making mothers look like they are lying.

If I had gone home straight away, I was certain I would have crumbled into depression. But divine help intervened through a phone call.

"Hi, Anna. Are you still there? Great. Don't leave until I visit you."

It was a family friend, Eve, a pediatrician working in the adjoining hospital. She came over and it was a blessing. She was the very first person to open up to me about the reality of motherhood. Up until that point, I thought I was weird or a failure because I was the only woman in the world not enjoying the experience.

Eve looked at me and said, "Don't be surprised if you feel like you want a refund." While that sounded horrific, I understood exactly what she meant.

She's cute. Don't be surprised if you feel like you want a refund.

She was saying it was all right to admit to yourself that sometimes motherhood was difficult, and in reallly, at times not so enjoyable. She wasn't going to beat herself up with guilt for having those feelings.

Eve continued, "If you feel that way, share it with your sisters, or close friends that will understand. Don't share it with just anybody because they will think you are nuts. If you really aren't coping, then get some help. Before you know it, Allegra will grow up and you will love her."

I felt so much better after her piece of advice. She was a pediatrician and loved children. She was a positive, wonderful person who gave advice to mothers, yet she also felt like getting a refund, just as her sisters felt. Her words gave me strength.

"Thank you."

If you do feel quite down after having a baby or feel like *actually* harming your child, go and seek professional help. The services available are amazing and can make such a difference.

We left the hospital with Allegra blissfully asleep in my arms. I relaxed during the full two hours she was asleep. While that seems like nothing to some people, I was celebrating.

It was a miracle for me.

Chapter 6

"I'm Here to Stay"

The first week that we brought Allegra home to our in-laws was another adventure in itself. Sheldon and I explored our new roles as parents, while Allegra turned our life upside down and back to front. It was a little bit like yoga for beginners. We were stretching in places we never knew we could, discovering newfound capabilities.

"Shhhhhhhhhhh...... Shhhhhhhhhh...... Don't wake up the baby.... Don't wake up the baby!"

I whisper-shouted at Sheldon and anyone within a fifty-yard radius as Sheldon transported her from the car. I was a crazy mommy, desperate to capitalize on this full two-hour sleep. Sheldon laid her gently in her bassinet. She was still the perfect Anne Geddes baby, all snuggled up, and blessedly asleep. No one would ever have guessed the torment from the week before.

Her sleep didn't last long. But it was enough for me to savor a short power nap. Once guests started visiting, analyzing her toes, her head, her eyes, and making comments, she was up once again. I thought, *Do you know what you have done? You have awakened the beast!*

"WAAAAAAAAAAAAAA!!!"

Although she was tiny, her scream sounded like it was amplified through huge speakers. Why did I bother getting two baby monitors? With a voice like that, she could be heard down the street.

No longer was I in the pre-baby world where Zen surroundings and tranquillity filled my day. It somehow got transferred into her world. Allegra was traveling first class, where all she needed to do was press that stewardess button – "WAAAAAHHHH!" – and I was promptly at her service. I was fitted with my stewardess uniform, a set of pajamas I wore 24 hours a day. Her scream was my alarm – a reminder that I was a feeding machine for my baby.

Sometimes, Sheldon would call me in a panic. "Quick, Anna. Feed her. Feed her! She's doing the 'Mariah Carey.' She's doing the 'Mariah Carey'!"

The "Mariah Carey" was the lip-quivering scream Allegra did that looked like she was punching out some big '90s ballad, complete with trills.

There was something different about Allegra. She was extremely alert, like she understood everything that was going on in the world. Even my aunties would comment, "It's like she's worked everything out." It was most likely because she was brewing up a plan for that evening.

The first night

There are a number of events in our lives that we will never forget. One of them was the second wedding proposal Sheldon made when the first proposal didn't quite cut it (the souvenir photo of the failed proposal is still sitting in our drawer). The second event was when Allegra slept with us for the first time at my in-laws'.

It started innocently. There was a heatwave and Allegra refused to go to sleep. No big surprise. Constant wailing occurred, so I picked her up and put her back down every five minutes. The only consolation was that I didn't have to go through it alone. Sheldon and I frantically fumbled through the night trying to find the one trick that worked.

"It's too hot!"

"No, no, no. It's too cold!"

"Use the fan instead."

"Perhaps she needs music?"

"Get soothing sounds, Get soothing sounds!"

We had quite an installation set up. The air-conditioning was set at an exact temperature, the fan was spinning at a twenty-degree angle, the lullaby music was selected on the laptop, and the freaking water fountain was plugged in, trickling with just the right portion of water.

"Nobody move."

It was a delicate operation. Silence followed, but it was soon disrupted.

"WAAAAAAAAAAAAAAAAHHHHHH!"

"Sheldon read the books. Read the books!"

The books were the set of sleep-settling emergency books with the guaranteed, full-proof methods to get babies to sleep. Sheldon picked one that had a perfect sleeping baby on the cover. He flipped through the chapters furiously.

"This one goes on and on about how full-proof the method is, but it doesn't actually tell you the method."

Sheldon picked up the other book and tried his best to settle Allegra without success. He flung the book across the room.

"NONE of this bloody works!"

Did the authors even deal with real babies when they wrote these books? We moved on to our third plan, which was a form of "musical beds." We moved her into our bed, her bed, a little travel bed, and even the bed in the spare room. At some point, she had pooped all over her clothes, my pajamas, the bedding, and the pillows.

The scene reached a climactic point when I was hosing her down in the bathroom at four in the morning while she screamed.

We had no idea what we were doing.

By the morning, the entire room looked like a wreck. Bedding and pillows were flung everywhere like a tornado had hit. Sheldon and I

had baby hangovers. The only one that didn't look like a wreck was little Miss Allegra, traveling in first class.

"I can't believe this little baby created so much havoc last night!" We pondered what we just experienced as we gazed at the cutest bundle sleeping innocently.

"What have we gotten ourselves into?" We were in for a long journey.

The "miracle" of motherhood

My mother-in-law had taken a couple of days off work to help me with our baby. This was part of our post-partum plan to assist with my lupus. It was the ideal situation and had definite benefits, such as enabling me to shower and eat. I was also able to catch up with relatives that lived nearby.

I reminisced about the days before Allegra was born. The days when all I longed for was a baby and nothing else mattered in the world. I recalled the shooting star, my miscarriage, and the lengths I went through to become pregnant.

I remembered the gyspy's prediction of my happiness and all the prayers we said each night to keep our baby alive. I remembered all those little conversations I had with Allegra in my tummy as I traveled to the Great Barrier Reef. All of this led me right back to this moment. I turned over to Sheldon.

"Put the baby back in my tummy."

The realization dawned on me that I was a better mother when Allegra lived inside me, not outside me. I was more loving, patient, and glowing. My hair looked better back then.

I opened my laptop and checked the congratulatory messages. The first was an e-card. Upon clicking, a fluttering baby with angelic wings pranced around the page beneath the words, "A little angel fell out of heaven." I couldn't understand why babies were pictured with angel wings when, clearly, they were capable of the opposite.

Another card had the message, "Dear Anna, How is the miracle of motherhood?" I said to myself, *The miracle is that we haven't put her up for adoption.*

I should have been grateful. I was aware that some parents were unable to have children and other babies were born with illnesses. But I allowed myself some sacred space where I gave myself permission to be truthful without feeling guilt or shame. Of course, I appreciated Allegra. I was just trying to find a way to cope with my transition to parenthood. Brutal honesty and humor was what got Sheldon and me through it.

I searched for reading material that revealed the reality of parenting. There was nothing in the local book store. I did, however, find one tiny article in a parenting magazine from a mother who shared the guts of parenting reality. I savored every little word like I was eating some exquisite chocolate because it simply made me feel better.

The start of the 25-year journey

We successfully survived the weekend and by Monday morning, Sheldon was getting dressed to go back to work. As he leaned over to say good-bye, I grabbed his shirt tightly, like a climactic scene from a thriller movie. "Don't go. Don't leave me alone with her. She's out to get me."

We made an arrangement that I would do most of the caregiving since we both wanted Sheldon to successfully complete his probation. Allegra was still sleeping, so I lay there in bed affirming myself. "It's okay, Anna. You can handle this. If single mothers can do it, you can do it."

I looked up toward the ceiling and took a deep breath. "I can do this. Just keep going until I get a break and..."

Something else dawned on me. There was no period in the near or distant future where I would get a break. This was not like other projects I had completed in my life where there was the prize of a finishing date. Allegra would be around for the next two weeks. The next five months. The next seven years. And the next twenty-five years! There was no handing Allegra over until the wedding day! Allegra was here to stay.

I did the calculations. She was now seven days old, so I had only begun the journey. If we organized an arranged marriage, I could

WEDDING DAY COUNTDOWN

2009

One day closer to the wedding.

possibly cut down the time frame. So I began the countdown to the wedding day. "She's one day closer to turning one. At least that would be one day I could cross out from the twenty-five years."

I glanced over at the bedroom wall where a collage of our Thailand honeymoon was hanging. There were images of scuba diving, water rafting, and hiking. All the pre-baby fun made me teary. There I was, grieving over my past life. "Fun, I miss you so much. Sniffle, sniffle."

Not quite butterflies

I heard that having children made you into a loving, fulfilled, and better person. I heard it expanded your heart and it brought a new dimension into your life. If this was the case, then I definitely knew there was an ugly in-between stage sandwiched between the creeping caterpillar and the beautiful butterfly.

In our case, we seemed to have turned into the worst human beings on the planet. Sheldon used to be the most patient man I had ever known. In fact, if you looked up the word "patience" in a dictionary circa 2008, his photo could have been there. He was labelled the "Golden Boy" at his previous firm, and was the personification of calm.

He rarely raised his voice. The women in his office loved sharing their personal dramas with him because he was wise beyond his years, offering sensible advice, never rash advice.

I never heard him swear. The most he would do when frustrated was let out one huge clap. "CLAP!" Strange, I know, but it was great for me as we rarely fought.

I, on the other hand, loved life. I loved dancing and I loved children. Parenthood was simply a new stage that would let me spread my wings and ascend to the sky.

After Allegra was born, I saw a whole other side of Sheldon's personality. Words I never knew he was capable of saying were flying out of his mouth. "F8%# this!" and "F*&% that!" spitted out left, right, and center. He even ran through red traffic lights in an effort to get the screaming baby home.

He was always a "mommy's boy," but now he was even antagonistic with his mother. There was a particular drama with the olive oil. Sheldon would smother Allegra in it and his mother would protest, "That's enough, Sheldon. You are putting on too much!" With heavy breathing, he would slowly stretch out his response with such guts and edginess.

"If I could, I would fill an entire bowl with olive oil and sit Allegra in it!"

Oh, boy. That was an intense moment. My eyes darted left and right to see who would fire the next arrow.

In my case, it was obvious how I had changed. I was broadcasting the worst aspects of parenthood to whoever was willing to listen. The neighbors, the postman, even the cat.

My mother had enough of it. "Don't be so negative."

How could she understand? Maids took care of us, as Mom and Dad traveled all over the world soon after giving birth.

I would seek sympathy. "Mom, I hardly had any sleep last night."

Then she would seek sympathy in return. "If you think that's bad, how about me? I hardly got sleep last night either."

"Yes, but that's because you played Scrabble until four in the morning."

I gave up seeking consolation from my mother. She was a Nazi when it came to empathizing with first-time moms. Instead, I turned to the Facebook world. Besides, I was doing a good deed. My stories were contraception for many people in the world.

I love you… I think

Many parents fall in love with their baby instantly. I think that is wonderful. In my case, falling in love took time.

I tried to say, "I love you" to Allegra. But it just wouldn't come out. We were like strangers. Like two people with mismatched personalities placed together in a room and told to live together with an instant connection.

I tried it again and again throughout the year. But every time I said, "I love you," another voice inside would counter it by saying, "You torture me." Looking back, I think it was the lupus. It was the feeling of aching, swollen joints from my neck to my toes. The only way to relieve that was sleep and, since sleep was not available, I was not an angelic mommy.

I felt relief when the visiting nurse said to me, "It's a myth that mothers instantly fall in love with their babies. While some do, many mothers need time to connect with their baby."

Years later, through life coaching, I learned to appreciate the wonderful uniqueness of Allegra. It took time for both of us to fall in love with her.

This is why I don't judge anyone who finds it hard to say, "I love you" from the very beginning.

Now I love saying it a hundred times a day, and I mean it.

Chapter 7

Most Babies vs. Allegra

Everyone tells you what newborn babies love before you even get to meet your little person. I rapidly discovered that nearly everything I was told by friends and professionals didn't apply to mine. Babies seemed to fall into two categories: all the babies in the world and Miss Allegra.

Newborn babies sleep most of the time

First, I was told by friends and professionals that newborn babies slept most of the time. They could barely stay awake in the beginning. In fact, the nurse I visited for sleep settling showed me the chart where Allegra was supposed to fit.

"According to this chart, Allegra should now be able to stay awake for one hour after every two hours of sleep."

Allegra was definitely off the charts.

"Yes, but Allegra is awake for six hours straight during the day screaming."

"Hmmm..." The well-meaning nurse gave me a half-pleasant smile, which meant, "Good Luck."

If only Allegra was content to be awake. Since she preferred to roar my mission was to get her down as soon as possible or feed her.

Newborn babies love baths

I watched a DVD that was part of our "Welcome to Parenting" pack. One part revealed how babies loved the soothing effect of water. It was supposed to remind them of being in the womb within the amniotic sac. When babies were unsettled, the super tip was to give them a bath.

"Here you go darling, enjoy your –"

"WAAAAAAHH!" She screamed like she was being tortured. Sheldon and I mastered the express baby wash in less than two minutes. After the traumatizing event, I'd lay there holding the hospital brochure, staring at the cover – a tranquil baby falling asleep in bubbles.

"You can tick that one off the list of favorite things."

Newborn babies love car rides

I was told babies loved car rides and that they fell asleep easily in car seats. The DVD even suggested when babies were irritable, a simple car ride would resolve the problem.

The baby car seat was like some sort of electric chair. Allegra would just scream. It stressed us so much we were afraid to drive anywhere. Sheldon tried his best to make the drive bearable by playing classical music. All that Mozart just made her red in the face. It became clear she wasn't a fan of traffic, either. The moment we were stuck, she cranked up the volume.

"Anna, let's meet up for coffee." A simple invitation from friends would trigger heart palpitations. Could we make it all the way? Eventually, I'd succumb to staying at home. Just playing the scene in my mind got me flustered.

The rule was a five-minute drive. If it was any more, I refused to get into the car. We almost gave ourselves a grand prize the day we endured an hour and a half trip to a wedding at Palm Beach. We said to the couple, "This is how much you mean to us."

Newborn babies love strollers

Could anything be further from the truth? Since I couldn't really drive anywhere, I innocently thought pushing Allegra in a stroller was an acceptable form of transport. Wrong.

"Forget the stroller, Mommy. Remember, I only travel first-class." That meant, carry only.

Weren't babies and strollers the inseparable pair, like the Olsen twins? I envied other moms who could contain their children under lockdown in their strollers.

"It's because you've just got to let her cry in the stroller and get used to it," my friends told me. I let her cry and was pretty sure at four months she said her first word – something all parents look forward to – in the stroller.

"Angar! Angar!"

It sounded a lot like "Anger." My friends thought I was joking, but Allegra looked pretty angry at the time.

Was it the brand or the color of the stroller? If so, we could resolve this methodically. We went through one, two, three strollers. I found myself talking to the strollers. "Don't worry. If Allegra won't have you, my parents' garage will. Dust will be your best friend."

I talked to inanimate objects a lot during that early stage. It's what happens to you when you are alone with a baby for nine hours a day. I'm pretty sure the walls spoke back.

At least we didn't spend a lot of money on the strollers. Friends offered me their wheels, and eBay was my best friend at the time.

Victory day arrived 18 months later, when Allegra finally gave the Maclaren stroller five stars. It was the first time she was content for more than five minutes. Hurray!

Newborn babies love baby swings, bouncers, or being rocked

My friend told me, "Anna, you are doing it all wrong. Your solution is to get a swing. My daughter was so unsettled and nothing would work until somebody gave us a baby swing. We'd leave her in there for hours."

I set out on a Fisher-Price mission and found a swing that took over the room like an amusement park ride. We placed Allegra inside, eagerly anticipating her reaction.

Her eyes said it all. "What do you think you are doing to me, people? WAAAHHH!"

The same applied to bouncers. She'd only last a few seconds. Why couldn't she be like my friends' babies who bounced and swung all day?

With such an array of things Allegra liked, no wonder our first local shopping trip was one to remember.

First, it took us one hour to pack and 30 minutes to find a parking spot. When we finally arrived, we dared to place Allegra in the stroller. Her megaphone scream instigated a series of synchronized head turns in the middle of the busy shopping center. The second shriek triggered the second tier of head turns from the upper floor. They probably thought we were starting a flash mob.

With the full circle staring at us, Sheldon panicked. "I can't handle this. Shopping for cotton balls is just too stressful! I'll do everything at work!"

It was the first time he had considered his stressful legal firm a place of tranquility. The entire shopping experience lasted five minutes. It would be months before we tried the great shopping centre challenge again.

There were things that Allegra did like.

Allegra liked pubs

Forget tummy time, bouncing, swinging, and playing with toys. Allegra was down for the pub.

The first time Allegra really settled was when we took her to a 30th birthday party in a crowded pub at Bondi Beach. It was completely inappropriate. Bodies bumped against each other, hands delicately balanced beers, and there were cheers and roars everywhere. We could hardly walk through the room.

It was like the fairy-pub-mother waved a magic wand and miraculously transformed Allegra into Sleeping Beauty. Amazing. We almost didn't make it. Her reckless one-hour scream in the car nearly made Sheldon do a U-turn. Fortunately, we persisted.

The same applied to loud parties. Since Filipinos are naturally loud, probably by physiology, that was easy. We just had to take her to a Filipino party. Onlookers would watch her sleeping in the middle of all the loud noise.

"Is she always this settled, Anna?" My response was evident through my deathly stare. Others questioned my stories. "You are such a liar. She can't possibly torment you."

So we did what all desperate parents did. We made sure our social calendar was completely booked back-to-back for at least a year. Now I only had to deal with the weekdays.

Allegra liked black Subaru Foresters

How old do you have to be before you can express your taste for cars? In Allegra's case, a couple of weeks into life.

At the time, we owned a red Toyota Corolla. While we owned that car, she clearly expressed her disapproval by shedding many tears. One time, I was waiting in the car with Allegra. She was screaming so loudly that strangers knocked on the window. "Hello? Is everything okay in there?" They thought she was an abandoned child or I was abusing her.

She cried and cried and cried until months later when we upgraded the car to a black Subaru Forester. We placed her in the car and she stopped crying. At 11 months of age, Allegra finally graced us with her blessing.

Allegra liked the Hug-a-Bub

I received a Hug-a-bub from my sister. It wasn't fancy. Just a long piece of fabric that wrapped around my body like a sling. It was the only item in my tool kit that worked. Since I had to carry her first-class constantly, it allowed me to function hands-free. That was fine at first. However, by the time she was nine months old, my back was breaking.

I received endless comments in public about this piece of fabric. If you do get it, but be prepared to stand in the middle of a parking lot, wrapping yourself like a mummy. It was not so easy on a rainy day.

What was the best benefit? It was great for boogying on the dance floor. When Allegra would not settle at weddings, I would strap her in and watch her drift to sleep while I did some dirty dancing.

Allegra liked Boyz II Men.

At some point during those first few months, Allegra was over the lullabies. After taking turns for four hours trying to put her to sleep, there was only one option left. Sheldon dug out the "old school" music.

Carrying her upright like a koala, he did his best rendition of the East Coast family while bopping to the beat. As soon as she fell asleep, Sheldon gently transferred her to the bassinette, but the screaming would begin.

"Don't you dare stop singing Boyz II Men, Daddy! And hold me straight!"

Despite singing the song, "End of the Road," there was no end in sight. Looking a little pale and needing an emergency toilet stop, Sheldon looked at me with eyes that yearned for saving. I'd look back at him, saying, "Don't look at me. She likes your voice better."

The diagnosis

Why was Allegra so different? Why did she scream so much?

Even my mother-in-law was worried and suggested I visit a family doctor to check for any problems. Allegra appeared to be fine, but she referred us to a paediatrician, just in case. Before I left, she gave me some advice.

"If you are having a difficult time, don't share it with people who have good, easy babies. They will say it has something to do with you. Share it with those people who have challenging babies." This was reassuring. She clearly understood what I had been through.

So I took Allegra to the pediatrician when she was three months old. After checking her, he gave me his verdict. "She appears to have colic."

My diagnosis: Your baby is a little bit challenging. That will be $230.

WAAAHHHH

What did that mean? "It doesn't mean anything, really. It is just a term we use for a baby that is very difficult."

Did I have to pay $230 to discover she was difficult? I already knew that!

He continued, "You just have to hang in there. Don't worry. Once she turns six months old, she'll be a completely new baby."

By then, I had received several promises of a "completely new baby." First it was five days, then three weeks, three months, and now six months. I was already in credit for at least three new babies. I think they knew that twenty-five years was too long, so bite-size goals made it bearable for me.

Baby credits:
They owe me
five new
babies.

five-day-old
three-week-old
three-month-old
six-month-old

Well, at least I knew nothing was physically wrong with her. So I tried everything available on the shelf for colic. Infant's Friend, gripe water, even the Cake Lady's Magic Liquid that she swore by.

Since nothing was working, I went to see a nurse named Elizabeth, and broke down crying in her office. She was one of the best nurses I ever dealt with.

"Look, your baby has got 'spark.' She is a little different than other babies because she is very alert. She is very clever. That 'spark' is going to take her places. It's going to be a huge benefit in the future. But, it in the meantime, it means it is going to be very, very challenging for you, as a mother, raising her."

80

She made me feel better by putting such a positive spin on Allegra's uniqueness.

She left me with one piece of advice before I left.

"In the future, when Allegra develops a cure for cancer, you can claim half the prize. You deserve it."

Congratulations. Your child has 'spark.'

Chapter 8

The M-Team

Mothers' groups are like wearing a bra. It's pretty uncomfortable, unless you find the perfect fit. Some mothers rave about the support they receive, while others find it restricting, preferring to go braless.

I understood Team Braless. I had friends who turned up to mothers' groups feeling no connection, listening to twenty women stretch time recounting their birth experiences. I even had a friend subtly kicked out of a mothers' group because she shared too many struggles. (They decided to change the venue without telling her.)

I also understood Team Perfect Support. Those were my friends who decreed mothers' group was the "wind beneath their wings." They still remained connected years later, celebrating weekends drinking wine at the Hunter Valley. For me, the experience was a little bit of both.

"Go join a mothers' group." That was the advice I was given by veteran mothers while I was pregnant. Somehow, in the cyclone of events after giving birth, that idea was swept away, along with the rest of my former life, to a faraway land called Oz. I had the intention, but there were obstacles. How would I join one? Did I just go to a park and try my best to pick up a mom, hoping she'd let me in on her posse?

Fortunately for me, in the midst of an Allegra crisis, a nurse named Taryn parted the great sea and made way to Mothers' Group Land.

"Anna, you should come to this group. You will quickly discover that there are so many mothers just like you going through the same tears and drama, and having the same Allegra issues."

"Just like me?" Within a second I paused my excessive sobbing. Using my inbuilt remote control system, I adjusted the brightness level to see a more positive picture of my life. I could actually feel a sparkle return to my eye. Just like me.

It was a group Taryn led at the community health center closest to my in-laws' house. Despite my fear of driving, I was willing to finally socialize with women who understood the grit and dirt behind the polished baby fallacy.

84

I packed my diaper bag and turned to my eight-week-old siren. "We are going to be part of this club whether you like it or not. So if you want to scream, then bring it on, baby!"

Mothers' Group: Take 1

The first 45 minutes of the meeting went well. I wasn't there. I was driving up and down the street, trying to find the address. "Curse you, 'No Right Turn' sign. Curse you!"

In the searing heat, I finally hit the brakes outside a little building that was not so easy to spot. Flustered, as usual, I quickly twisted my mommy wrap, slipped Allegra inside, and bolted through the door.

What did I see?

It was like a scene from Wisteria Lane. The women looked cool, collected and well-groomed as they sat in their circle. The twenty strollers were parked perfectly, like a fleet of Rolls Royces on display in a showroom, with accessories. Each baby lay in its stroller or in its mother's arms, glowing and radiant.

There were no babies screaming. Instead, twenty pairs of eyes were looking my way. I felt like I had crashed a high tea. Women looked like they were perfect croissants and one lady reminded me of English breakfast tea. I, on the other hand, was more like scrambled eggs.

My dishevelled hair was all over my face. My dull eyes with matching eye bags peered through the strands of my greasy hair. My stained clothing, which I had hastily shoved on, was part of my Autumn 2009 Blemished Collection. My friend would later refresh my memory. "Oh Anna, I remember you. You looked like a mess every time you turned up at mothers' group."

Since I arrived in the last ten minutes of the meeting, Sharon invited me into the spotlight. "Would you like to share anything, Anna?"

Feeling quite vulnerable in front of a group of flawless women I didn't know, I took the plunge and poured out all the dramas I could fit within three minutes. The meeting wrapped up soon after.

I didn't feel a connection to the group, although Taryn was fantastic and welcomed me. Perhaps it was the structure. Something felt unnatural about sitting in a big circle with a wide-open space in the middle. It could have also been because Allegra was the only baby who wouldn't sit in a stroller. I was at least hoping for some comradeship in the stroller-less department.

Not all was lost. Before I left, there were snippets of hope as some friendly mothers glanced my way with a smile. So I decided to return the following week. Even though I couldn't relate to the women, it was better than talking to the walls.

The following week, I understood how the mothers' group system worked. Taryn facilitated the circle as women took turns sharing what they had been through.

"How has your baby been this week?"

"My baby hardly ever screams," one mother shared. I couldn't help but notice how easy it was for other mothers.

Another mother confided, "My baby sleeps through the whole night."

I kept thinking, *Please share more struggles and make me feel normal.*

Taryn finally turned to me. "Anna, would you like to share any-thing?"

As usual, I opened the floodgates and blurted out everything. "My baby screams all day and all night. I can't even get her into a stroller. We've taken her to doctors, but nothing is technically wrong with her!" It was like I had a perfectly functioning toy except the toy had a mind of its own, or was possibly possessed by a dramatic spirit.

I went on. "From the moment she entered the earth, she's been the biggest challenge of my life. My life has fallen apart. I feel like a mess. I'm not even meant to be here. I'm meant to be at home, but I'm afraid to be left alone with her, so I'm still at my in-laws' house. I'm afraid!"

I didn't mind being the odd one out – I knew I had to get it off my chest. Afterwards, mothers continued their pleasant sharing. True, some women had minor struggles, but nowhere near the catastroph-ic news I shared week by week.

Don't get me wrong. I knew the importance of switching from negative thinking to positive thinking. I was always a let's-look-at-the-positive-side type of girl. But there was something therapeutic about speaking the truth instead of suppressing feelings then resenting my baby even more. I didn't filter my words by trying to sound more pleasing or acceptable.

Another week, Taryn posed the question, "Can you share your experience of motherhood? Is it better or worse than you expected?"

One wide eyed mother eagerly put up her hand. "Motherhood is even better than I expected. I was never into children or babies, but after having mine, it became better than I expected."

I dared to put up my hand, making my blasphemous statement, "It is worse than I expected! I always loved babies before. I was a better mother before I had a baby. I can't sleep, I can't settle her, I am attached to her, and it's not the experience I dreamed of. Put the baby back in my tummy!"

I don't remember anyone else sharing after that. Nevertheless, I liked the group. It was all I had, even if I couldn't relate to them.

Lingering

Each week, I carried out my exciting routine after mothers' group – filling the car with gas. You could always tell which car was mine. It was always the crying car. Strangers would look my way and I would politely reply, "New baby inside."

I didn't want to go home as it would depress me, so I did my other activity, lingering. Lingering was when I would hang out for a few hours at a local mall to remain sane. I did try shopping initially, but after racking up a big credit card bill from retail therapy, I decided lingering was a safer option.

As I aimlessly carried Allegra around Kmart, I noticed Amanda, one of the mothers from my mothers' group who had exchanged friendly glances with me. She was pushing a stroller back and forth, sipping her Wendy's Frosty, doing her own lingering.

"Hey." We both laughed, realizing we were in the same boat, trying to get through the day. So I invited her over and we had a couple of

The art of lingering...

hours of deep sharing about our lives. It really helped me to know there was another mother who lived close by. I wasn't opening myself up to a group of women I hardly knew. She became my first new mother friend. It was like I was back at school and I had finally met a person willing to share her lunchbox with me. Amanda had a brilliant career, but really wanted a child and now had to through the same challenges I was experiencing.

The following week, after mother's group, Amanda pulled me aside and told me something that made me feel normal for once. She was so honest. "We need to talk. I accidently dropped a pile of plates the other day."

I never realized how one sentence could provide such relief. Dropping plates? Someone else experienced the same stress and anxiety that I was going through on a daily basis. I wasn't alone. Her next words became the opening door to my salvation.

Mothers' Group: Take 2

"Anna, do you want to come over to my house? I'm having my own little mothers' group with a group of moms I met at a workshop."

I showed up at Amanda's house with Allegra and recognized some familiar faces. There were other friendly moms who had smiled at me from the larger mothers' group, plus some new faces.

We lay our babies in a row on the floor and relaxed on the couch with our coffee, tea, and chocolate cake. It felt different being there – it was comfortable. I felt an instant connection and a trust with the group, and there no formalities but rather heart-to-heart conversations. I felt I could share my struggles there without a circle of women sitting on chairs, looking at me like I was an alien.

I started conversing with a new mother I met, and asked her, "How is motherhood for you?"

Her name was Nicole. She had a warmth about her, was kind, and she looked like she had it all together and under control. So I was surprised with her answer.

"Sometimes she would continue screaming so much, I wouldn't want to leave my room. There were even times I was crossing off weeks on my calendar for each week I survived."

Hurray! I wasn't rejoicing over her struggles. I was relieved I finally found a group where women could open up realistically.

"What about your birth experience?" I asked. "Did you get the magic moment?"

Nicole looked at me and said, "I was more excited that my food arrived than my baby."

Mmm... food.

I was so grateful for the honesty. We continued to gather week by week as we watched our babies grow. There was so much healing that came with sharing honestly and having friends there who identified with or supported you. It made the road easier to bear.

These women became my core group – my support team – the "M" team. They were like bodyguards, armed with machine guns ready to defend each mother's self-esteem and self-worth through support and love whenever the babies really pushed our buttons.

I can justly say this heroic team helped me tremendously during the first three years of motherhood. Because of these women, I actually enjoyed moments of motherhood. The larger mothers' group eventually dissembled. Although I didn't relate to them, I was grateful for the experience because I wouldn't have met these amazing women without it.

So my verdict is mothers' group can work – even if it takes a couple of rounds. When I moved back home to Croydon, I tried to find a local mothers' group. Apart from seeing my close friends with babies, I wanted a support group closer to home. I came close when I asked a mother for her contact number. In the end, I didn't mind to keep driving the long distance to see my M-team.

Today, we continue to celebrate together. We just had our fourth Mothers' Group Christmas party. Of course, now there is the second round of babies, including new twins. Except, err, for Sheldon and me.

But that's another story.

Chapter 9

Baby Boot Camp

It was like a scene from the reality show, "The Biggest Loser." We were on a four-day baby boot camp, learning how to tame the beast and regain control of our lives. These nurses were the toned, fearless trainers who did not heed to the cry of a baby – the cry that would normally send parents buckling.

The trainers pepped us up. "Who's the boss? You are. Will you let this four-month old manipulate you? No!"

Okay, it wasn't quite like that, but it felt like it.

So how did we end up at this baby boot camp? It all began a week after Allegra was born.

"We are coming over. That baby sounds like it is torturing you." It was my colleague Miranda on the phone. She and her husband were starting to worry about Allegra's impact on me. It felt comforting to know I had bodyguards ready to save me, but I didn't want to inconvenience them.

Instead, Miranda put me in touch with a friend named Emily who did some work with an amazing parenting organization. This Family Care Center provided expert parenting advice for newbies like me. Prior to meeting her, I had no idea they even existed.

Emily invited me to her house when Allegra was nine days old. She and her husband Jim were a kind couple who participated in a fostering program. They volunteered to care for babies in the interim period before they settled in a foster home.

"This is Joseph. He's only five weeks old, and we are minding him at the moment."

I couldn't believe how easy Joseph was. He played on his tummy (without screaming) and drank his bottle (without screaming). When it was sleeping time, Emily placed him in his crib, put the radio to static, and walked away. He fell asleep on his own (again, without screaming). He probably had gentle DNA, not the erratic DNA Allegra was composed of.

"Can I swap babies?" It was like the Universe was playing a joke on me.

My chiropractor later described it to me this way. "Of all people, you probably need the most rest with your lupus and, instead, you got the child with the most energy and drama."

Emily assured me, "Just follow the steps I will show you and try to stick to a routine." I revved myself up, ready to dive into the challenge when Allegra decided to play another trick on me.

"Oh, look. She's sleeping." Of all places, why did she have to fall asleep when I was about to get professional help? I had described a monster and now she was an angel. She eventually did this Jekyll-and-Hyde plan every time I sought sleep-settling assistance. I sat around for the rest of my time, playing with my thumbs.

The Mother Ship

At least Emily didn't leave me to fend for myself. Before leaving, she gave me her number and eventually wrote me a referral for a day visit to the mother ship – the Family Center headquarters. There was usually quite a waiting list, but I was fortunate to get an appointment when Allegra was three weeks old. Emily must have ticked the "mother on the verge of going nuts" box on the form.

The day of the appointment was one I would never forget. My mother drove us while Allegra shrieked her latest version of the 'Mariah Carey" for an entire 45 minutes. Had her voice grown stronger? She must have upgraded her amplifier.

My mother always had an extremely loud voice. So much so, even a deaf person could hear her. This is why Sheldon blamed my side of the genes for creating Allegra's scream.

Being the disciplinarian, my mother thought she could control Allegra by raising her voice in the car.

"Screaming is NOT allowed!"

Allegra would scream louder like she was saying, "I'll do as I darn please!"

It was a competition between the vocal chords. But even the mighty strength of my mother was no match for Allegra. My mother accepted her defeat.

We arrived at our appointment, sat inside a room, and met Megan, the kind nurse who would take care of us.

"So tell me what's happening with Allegra."

I began expanding on my elaborate three-week drama, including the screaming and lack of sleep. In the midst of rambling, we both looked at Allegra. Yep, she had fallen asleep within the first five minutes of my day visit. She looked like a little koala bundled up snuggly.

"Why does she do this to me? Why?"

We placed Allegra in a crib. Apart from feeding, she basically slept soundly for the entire day – something she had never done at home of course. Was it the thread count of the crib sheets? You could never underestimate Allegra's particular preferences for such things.

There was nothing else for me to do except listen to the steps of settling a baby "in theory" and to fill out a questionnaire.

One of "them"

Back in the days when I was pregnant and glowing, I asked my pregnant friend a question. "What's postnatal depression?"

I never really found out because she replied by saying, "Don't worry about that, Anna. That will never happen to you! You are such a positive, bubbly person."

So I never worried about it. Though I did question why women would feel the need to be depressed when they had such a bundle of joy in their lives. Couldn't they just get over it? I narrowed it down to having too much spare time to think of negative thoughts.

On the contrary, I soon discovered it was having too little time, too little sleep, too little of everything women used to have, that could lead to the baby blues or depression. I never would have imagined I'd be one of them.

I filled out the questionnaire which surveyed how I was coping with motherhood. My result was mild-postnatal depression. With all my stories, I was expecting something worse. I could finally understand the women I had initially judged. In fact, I couldn't comprehend how women did not get some form of depression from sleep deprivation alone.

They set me up with a counselor. She was brilliant and understanding. I poured out and vented all my frustrations over a number of appointments, knowing I wasn't sounding like a broken record as I did with friends and family. I could share with her without being hushed.

Before leaving, the nurse gave me her number as a life line. I collected Allegra, who turned back into her usual self as she screamed merrily all the way home in the car. I should have camped there, as I would return when Allegra was five weeks, three months, four months, seven months, and thirteen months old. I was a Family Care Center addict.

In the meantime, I called Megan whenever I needed. "What do I do? She's still screaming."

"Take her for a walk outside in the park – people won't hear her."

So I would do just that only to receive comments from strangers. "Was that your baby? I could hear her screaming from across the field."

I had a number of friends who gave birth that same year. And most of them were easier-going babies. You knew you had a challenging baby if your friends who just gave birth apologized for having an easy one.

I'd ask, "How's your baby?"

They'd respond, "He's really easy going. Sorry."

When Allegra reached three months of age, it became tougher. The moment I'd drift off to sleep, Allegra would wake me for a feeding every two hours. Once she was fed and asleep, I would be wide awake. Our cycles were completely out of sync. The sun would rise after a total of 15 minutes of sleep and we would repeat the same process.

I added extra tools to my belt by joining baby workshops, baby massage, other sleep settling sessions – anything that could possibly help me. Eventually, Allegra consumed me.

"Help!" I gasped.

Thankfully, Megan picked up my S.O.S. and decided on some priority action. It was time to turn it up a notch. It was time to call in the big guns – baby bootcamp.

We were going to straighten out this little lady and regain control of our lives. Allegra had been running the show, but a new era would begin where she would have to surrender and wave that little white flag.

Who's the boss, baby?

One of my favorite forms of vacationing is going on a cruise ship. There's definitely something about the fresh air, the organized itinerary of fun, not having to worry about cleaning or entertainment, and having food delivered around the clock.

The baby boot camp or "live-in" experience is a lot like a cruise ship vacation. That is, if you exchange the buffets and a la carte with hospital food, music and entertainment with a collection of screaming babies, and the cleaning service to do-it-yourself. Apart from that, having a team of nurses settling your baby for a full day while you watched behind the safety of a glass window felt much like breathing fresh air on a ship deck. Glorious! There were other perks; you received your own hotel-style room and one night on a date with your partner while they babysat.

People warned me that these women were ruthless when it came to controlled crying. If they couldn't sort your baby out, no one could! Sheldon and I settled into our room where we would stay for the next four nights until checkout.

Along the corridors, I could hear wailing and screaming from young babies to older toddlers. There were worn-out mothers and fathers, and even parents with twins.

As I grabbed a coffee, I listened to the amazing before-and-after story from one mother checking out. "My toddler was 'Chucky' from the movie 'Child's Play,' and now he has changed completely, thanks to the nurses."

I was thrilled at the thought of a makeover. We'd put Allegra in one end of the boot camp and she would pop out on the other side new and improved. The parents would also get a makeover, from weaklings to muscle parents. There was nothing physically wrong with Allegra – I knew that. But I felt guilty if I didn't pick her up every time she cried, and this was wearing me out.

Lesson 1: Teach your baby to self-soothe.

"It's all about self-soothing. Teach your baby to put herself to sleep. You do not pat your baby to sleep. You pat her to reassure her, and then you leave. After a few minutes, if her screaming escalates, you can return to reassure her but you must leave again."

We quickly understood the process of the makeover. We had to toughen up and not give in to every little squeak from Allegra. She was relying on us, unable to fall asleep by herself. It was our own fault. We made ourselves her slaves. We felt like we had graduated the first module of our training.

Allegra knew something had changed, and she didn't like it one bit. Her scream escalated, escalated, and escalated. Thank goodness for the glass window that protected our ears from her soundwaves. It was definitely a match between the nurses and the baby. Sheldon and I watched from our front-row seats. Allegra was winning 40 – love.

Six hours later, one nurse thought she finally had Allegra down as she became silent for a few seconds. In slow motion, the nurse turned the corner and slowly lifted her heel. Her shoe picked up a miniscule piece of sticky tape.

"Rrrrrrippppp."

"WAAAAAAAAAAAAAAAAAAAAAAAAAAAHHHH!"

The nurse rolled up her sleeves. "Hmm. Tough cookie. She is extra-alert. Don't worry. By the end of this, she'll give in."

Lesson 2: Listen to the Cry

The next piece of advice sounded a little odd. "Now I want you to listen to her cry."

"But I listen to her cry all the time."

"No. Not just listen. Really listen to her cry." We looked at the nurse inquisitively. "If the gap of silence between each scream lengthens, then she is closer to falling asleep on her own. If it shortens, then you may need to go to her and reassure her with some pats."

The nurse's wise words hit us like an ancient proverb. She was like Yoda giving advice to us young Jedi masters. We were using "The Force," all these seeds of wisdom to improve our relationship with our baby. We had the power within us.

So Sheldon and I spent our days fine-tuning our listening skills. By the end, I felt like David Attenborough, able to distinguish even the mating calls of bird species. The only mating call I wouldn't pick up was my husband's. I refused to go down that path again.

Listen...

Lesson 3: Don't let her fall asleep

"Don't allow Allegra to fall asleep at the wrong time." The next piece of advice sounded odd, but we didn't question it.

"Yes, sensei."

The nurse explained why. "Micro-sleeps are the most dangerous. If she gets even a few seconds of micro-sleep when she is meant to be awake, that will give her enough of a re-charge to keep fighting without sleep. She will then skip the next deep sleep and continue screaming."

Allegra was a self-charging battery. We were FBI agents on a mission to extinguish her resource and secret weapon – the micro-sleep. It was already the second day. Allegra had spent the first day and a half refusing to self-settle. Since she missed another sleep, the nurse gave us the signal. "Keep her awake until the next scheduled sleep at 16:00."

We had two hours to spare, so I innocently suggested a short walk to the store to buy some Milo. All was well until we saw the dangerous blinks from Allegra's eyes, followed by plenty of silence. The drama ensued as Sheldon started panicking, forcing me to load the groceries on the conveyor belt quickly. He was distressed, blaming me for putting her at risk.

"Stupid Milo." We nearly got divorced over it.

"Try something! Shake her!"

We were at the checkout, swinging Allegra side to side in the air like a pendulum, as we paid by credit card. It was a tragedy. "She's falling asleep! She's falling asleep!" People thought we were nuts. Her eyes were comfortably closed and she even had a slight grin.

We ran as fast as the stroller would let us, back in time for her next scheduled sleep. There we were, panting out of exhaustion. Allegra got the better of us – she had her micro sleep! Now she was wide awake.

Hope

As we failed our first micro-sleep mission, Allegra was roaring again during her next sleep session. But, by the evening, we finally had our first sign of hope. After nearly two days, she finally settled by herself.

Her self-settling statistics showed improvement over the course of the boot camp. For the first two days, it took a day and a half of screaming to self-settle. By the third day, it took three hours, and by day four, she was down to one hour.

Hallelujah! She fought, but we finally won. We vowed to continue the process. I thanked the boot camp nurses for all their hard work and patience. And I recommended their program to anyone who would listen.

In the end, I finally had the strength to take over. I was super-confident and happy to reclaim my life. For the first time as a mother, I let her scream, and happily read Stephanie Meyer's "Twilight" series, putting my feet up.

Order was restored to my universe and we were no longer getting a divorce over Milo. This led to Sheldon and me moving Allegra into her own room and reclaiming our space. With my new method of sleep training, I eventually scheduled all my activities – household chores, cooking, and so forth, with ease. I would place Allegra into bed screaming, while I enjoyed a soothing, hot shower.

I finally had the courage to say to Sheldon, "It's time to move back home. We're in control now, baby."

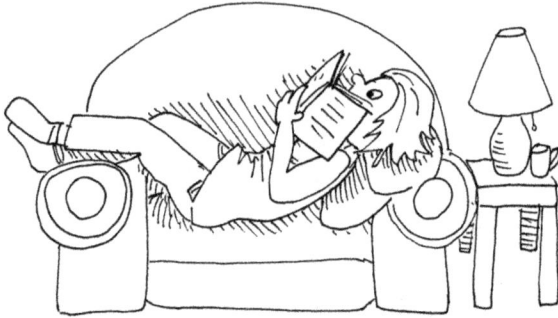

Chapter 10

The Hunger Games

We finally reached the "Golden Age," the momentous moment when Allegra would graduate to solid foods. This can be quite an exciting time for new parents. That is, as long as your baby doesn't decide to go on a hunger strike. Just because we moved out and had Allegra's sleep-settling under control, it didn't mean all was breezy. She planned other ways to even up the score.

For the first six months, Allegra and I were an unstoppable breastfeeding team. At the time, I heard so many challenging breastfeeding stories I could have dedicated an entire chapter to the topic. But, in our case, it went surprisingly well. Breastfeeding was convenient for me mainly because I didn't have to sterilize bottles. I chose not to get involved in the breastfeeding vs. bottle debate, and stuck close to my motto, "Do whatever works for you."

At around six months of age, the hunger games were inaugurated. It was war – literally. But how did it all begin?

Food Fantasy

Like all my baby war stories, it began with a fantasy.

Friends prepared me for a wonderful experience. "Allegra is such a great eater. She is always hungry. It's a sign that she really wants to move on to solids. She's going to gobble those solids down."

The fantasy evolved into organics as people gave me more advice.

"Don't give her the bottled foods. They are packed with preservatives."

"Cook the food yourself and make sure you use organic fruits and vegetables, and your baby will love it."

I imagined myself as an organic, wholesome, home-cooked-food mommy. I chopped, boiled, and blended my ingredients, pouring my purees into ice cube trays for portion control. I cooked soups, fruits, and sauces. I basically cooked anything that grew out of the earth, while singing Willy Wonka's song, "Pure Imagination." Just like the scene in the movie when the children were fascinated by the magical land of sweets, Allegra would be awe-struck by my wonderful world of organics. I know, a little bit far-fetched.

I also introduced a new law in our Garcia constitution: Allegra would not eat any sugar, salt, or preservative, or watch the visual preservative, television. Once reality set in, the entire constitution was tossed out the window and replaced by the ruling, "Feed her whatever will stay in her mouth." If she didn't projectile vomit or spit food out, it passed.

Part B of the law was also amended to read, "The children's channel is your best friend." It came in handy when I was losing the plot. As long as there was no porn, gun-shooting, or F-words, television got the stamp of approval.

Fast-forward a couple more years to toddlerhood, when Allegra would simply bypass food altogether and request a grain of salt on her plate.

"Allegra, what would you like for dinner?"

"Mommy, I'd like to have one salt, please."

Refusing to offer the salt banquet would often lead to something even more tragic. Allegra would dig for gold up her nose and cunningly slip into her mouth the second I glanced the other direction.

"Don't do that! That's disgusting!"

"But it's salty, Mommy! I love salt."

The other challenge we faced was all the children's parties we attended every weekend, along with the matching accessory – the party bag!

Party bags were simply bags of sugar contrived into a hundred colorful forms of all shapes and sizes. We got so accustomed to them that the moment we received the bag, Sheldon's eyes would light up, eager for first picking.

"What did we get this time?"

I managed to hide 95% of the lollipops from both Allegra and Sheldon.

So there we were, in our house, ready to give Allegra her first bite of food – baby rice cereal – at six months of age. Her first swallow was a major accomplishment. We cheered and clapped.

"Good girl, Allegra. Since you are being so good, soon I will give you more colorful food."

But there was one concern we had.

Allegra was no longer pooping. We were anxious and distressed. I hung on the helpline, seeking the advice of a nurse.

"She's just adjusting to solids. Don't worry it will come. Just give her some prune juice and grease her behind with a bit of Vaseline."

In my former life, Vaseline was something used for chapped lips in the winter. Now we were using it to grease a baby's butt. I could never bring Vaseline back in contact with my lips after that.

A week later, while Sheldon was holding her chubby legs in the air, it all erupted like a volcano. An avalanche.

Welcome to the world of solids.

All appeared to be going swell, but three weeks after starting solids, Allegra decided enough was enough. Her face said it all. "I shall now declare that I am on a solids strike for six months."

For the first few weeks, I thought she was just adjusting. Surely she would turn around? Surely she would get hungry? But, after attending my mothers' group and seeing other babies her age transitioning easily into solids, I once again called for help by visiting the health center.

ℱinely tuned tastebuds

By that point, I must have seen or spoken to every nurse in Sydney. Karyn was one of the exceptional ones. She delicately explained why Allegra wasn't eating.

"That's because the food you are offering is not tasty enough. Would you eat it?"

I thought about that. "No, not really."

"She has finely tuned tastebuds. She wants a cuisine. Give her something amazing."

I didn't realize Allegra had such a penchant for five-star dining. Obviously, rice cereal and pureed pumpkin were below the benchmark. Would I be able to whip up something that appeased her palate?

Karyn handed me a booklet. It was a recipe book for fussy eaters. "Make her a delicious omelette, or how about French toast? Experiment a little. Have some fun."

I went home with renewed hope and got the hot plates fired up. With such vigour, I had four different meals cooking at once. I chopped with one hand, sprinkled herbs with another, multi-tasking like Jamie Oliver. Even my neighbors questioned my tantalizing feast.

The Food Critic

After hours of work, I spooned a small amount of each into Allegra's mouth. Like a food critic, she paused, thinking about the textures and the flavors, before giving me her slamming judgement: "WAAHHHH" which meant "No, no, no, and NO!"

Okay, so I wasn't the Iron Chef, but surely she could work with my limited culinary skills? I just wasted hours in the kitchen brewing large stews, omelettes, and French toast. Sheldon became my disposal unit, forced to eat Allegra's meals.

I attended parties and watched as mothers spoon-fed entire bowls of pureed vegetables easily to their babies. Gone were the days when I envied people's mansions, cars, or Tiffany rings. Now I simply envied mothers with munching babies.

"I wish my baby would eat food the way your baby does."

The mother looked at me, proud of her accomplishment. "That's because I cook all my own food."

I felt my nose flare as I turned to the oblivious mother. "Let me tell you, it's not always about the mother. Babies can be picky, too!

Babies can be..." I had to think for a moment, "...possessed by an anti-eating beast." I didn't really say this, rather a milder version of it. I was passionate about clearing the myth that home-cooked food guaranteed consumption.

The Food Artist

As a former Visual Arts teacher, I knew the time it took to produce fully resolved artworks from conception to the finished work. In Allegra's case, she could create an original artwork in well under sixty seconds. She used her creative genius to spray, splat, and throw food everywhere except the target – her mouth. Later, she created these masterpieces at the most timely moment; just minutes before I was leaving for work.

I purchased a three-metre piece of plastic, which I tediously rolled out every mealtime to shield my poor furniture. That accompanied three full-length protective feeding suits that looked like she was ready to go into space. Even my messy-eating friends started to ask me, "Wow. Do they sell those in adult sizes?"

My preventive measures were no match for my modernist artist. She'd simply exceed the boundary of the plastic, creating a Jackson Pollock masterpiece all over the walls and furniture within a 360-degree, five-yard radius.

If I could have sold tickets to the arty crowd, they could have entered my house and experienced Allegra's original installation.

"It's very avant-garde for the baby world," they would probably say, drinking their posh wine.

Most of the furniture survived, except for our large couch and dining seats, which eventually met their fate out on the street for collection.

The IKEA chair

I later directed my fury to the high chair. Maybe it carried the wrong energy. Just like the stroller, I bought another one, and another one, and finally a Bumbo seat. If I placed it in the right direction, maybe it would magically transform the food into something appetizing. It could have worked in a Harry Potter book, but in Allegra's world the magic dwindled as she screamed, refusing to stay in any chair.

"Sheldon, please add the chair to her growing 'Don't Like' list."

I'll tell you how the magic did work. The food was magically transported and wedged into the most unreachable crevices of all her seats. There, it solidified like concrete. There was only one thing left to do.

"Call Crissy. We are getting the IKEA high chair."

Crissy had offered it to me from the beginning, but I was too proud and refused it under aesthetic grounds. I eventually succumbed to the power of the IKEA chair, notably its ease of cleaning, and came begging at her door, as she predicted.

Some words of advice – don't play musical chairs. Drive straight to IKEA, get yourself a cart, and walk straight to the baby section.

It's deceivingly simple, but it may spare you from pulling your hair out when you can't remove the solidified food sculpture growing on your chair.

The Grand Canyon

I started talking myself out of feeding her solid foods. I suppose this was part of her game play. Possibly Allegra could survive on a diet of breastfeeding. She could be in the "Guinness Book of World Records" as the only human adult sustained on a diet of breast milk.

After all, breastfeeding did have its pros. Before I became pregnant, I was as flat as an ironing board. I was pretty sure I had a negative bra size and could have been cast in the "Itty Bitty Committee." Breastfeeding gave me just enough curves so I could sing Whitney Houston's song, "I'm Every Woman." I wasn't ready to return to the men's club.

I could get away with it. I pictured Allegra age twenty, still hanging off me. No, it wasn't a pretty picture. She had to make the transition to solids.

Just for the record, my curves deflated back to oblivion, minus another cup size. I was already flat before Allegra, and now I became the Grand Canyon.

I turned toward Allegra's resources, showing her a picture of the Cookie Monster, and I slowly pronounced my words. "Do you see this, Allegra? It's what human beings do. They eat. Munch, munch, munch. Want to try?"

The special menu couldn't do it, the high chair couldn't do it, and even the Cookie Monster couldn't do it.

So I went back to see Karyn and burst out crying again. As Allegra was also unsettled and screaming a lot, Karyn organized a counselor to visit me at home for the next four months, and also put me in touch with a charity organization. They arranged for a volunteer to relieve me for two hours every two weeks for about six months. The volunteer, Jennifer, was extraordinary with Allegra. All of this was to relieve the stress and assist my lupus.

Karyn gave me one more piece of advice.

"Just feed her what you are eating. Don't make a special meal for her. Break off a bit of what you are eating."

I did that and it worked. I would sit with my mothers' group, watching them feed their babies healthy vegetables and fruit. They would turn to me asking, "What's Allegra eating?"

"You know, green curry, tofu, mungo beans, and a cookie that says it should be for three-year-olds."

"Allegra always has to be different."

Snail eating

Imagine your child holding a cookie. Now imagine your child eating ten crumbs of that cookie. Finally, imagine your child eating those ten crumbs over two hours, but relying on you to spoon-feed each crumb. Do you understand the kind of psychological damage this could do to a parent? Yes, she was finally eating, but eating like a snail.

I sat there, spoon-feeding her rice, gazing hazily into the distant future – a year of two-hour-long feeding sessions, three times day. I think I shed a tear. Anna, this is going to be a long painful journey.

I stared at my daughter. Since most of the rice had landed all over her, Allegra had turned into a lamington (an Australian coconut-covered chocolate cake).

Another boot camp?

I couldn't function like this, so I decided to call in Special Forces. Within no time, I was back for another day visit with the Family Care Center.

"What seems to be the issue?" She was a strong nurse, not willing to take any manipulative action from Allegra. As I spoke, she filled out the forms. It was Allegra's nap time, so I decided to settle her while the nurse waited. This turned into a massive drama and gave the nurse more to scribble on her form. She sounded the words as she filled it out. "Issues with feeding, self-settling... Well, just about everything. Anna, I'm worried about you."

"I'm worried about me, too."

On top of everything, Allegra was also teething.

"I'd like to see Allegra two more times and if she doesn't improve, she may need to do another live-in program at around thirteen months old."

Another boot camp? Was I regressing?

I explained the history of the hunger games.

She responded with wisdom. "Ignore her."

Okay, I wasn't expecting that.

She continued. "Why should she eat when she is enjoying a spectacular show? All of your reactions to her not eating are entertaining. The more you make a big deal, the less she will eat. The more you ignore her, the more likely she will eat."

It made perfect sense. But she was so young. Could she contrive such a plan? We did a test run and ignored her as instructed. I turned my back and allowed my peripherals to analyse her actions. After a few minutes, she started munching away. Unbelievable!

The nurse gave me one more tip in regards to her snail eating. "Give her a time limit, and then pack up. She will get the message quickly. Don't worry. She won't starve."

Ignoring her was the easiest piece of advice I was given. We finally put an end to the Hunger Games. I was breathing fresh air again and celebrating this victory. Allegra turned one, and I was happy to cross off her first out of twenty-five years.

She eventually grew to love food, especially cooking, and even served up her own interesting feasts.

In fact, if you ever get the privilege to dine with Allegra's plastic tea set, she will ask you the essential question, "Do you want chocolate salt with your tea?"

"Yes, ma'am."

Chapter 11

"Honey...I Think we Have a Diva"

Since the beginning of time, man has asked fundamental questions surrounding humankind's existence. Why are we here? Where are we going? And the most important of all, where did the diva come from?

Some postulate Allegra's diva-dom began at the tender age of two, when exposure to hours of Disney princess movies infiltrated her brain and put her neurological diva cells into overdrive. Others propose genealogy as the origin, attributing it to the passing of the genes from the great diva ancestors.

I, on the other hand, believed Allegra's diva nature was crafted with ingenuity in the first weeks of cell life within my womb, as part of a master plan to test Sheldon and my limits.

There was always the mystery surrounding her existence. One nurse suggested I conceived twins, yet only one survived. This could explain the unexpected test results that suggested a miscarriage.

Sheldon supported such a theory. "I wouldn't be surprised if Allegra, you know, bumped the other one off. There's only room for one of us in this world!'"

After all, a diva was a prima donna and the leading lady in a performance. Her audience was the world, and she was preparing for her big debut. I typed the word "diva" into Google, and summarized a list of traits that matched Allegra exactly.

A diva:
- Had attitude
- Had confidence
- Had lots of personality
- Exuded style
- Had a temper
- And got exactly what she wanted or no way at all.
- Believed everyone was beneath her.

Wikipedia could even stick an image of Allegra under the word "diva." She could play the role of Veruca Salt in a prequel.

The early signs

There were early signs that showed she was different from others her age, and much more cunning. At the age of 18 months, Allegra had the natural ability to get herself out of blame. When I heard her pass wind like a trumpet and asked, "Did you just fart, Allegra?" her answer was blatant.

"No." She pointed to her fabric doll. "She did."

At twenty months, she would cry in the middle of the night. Sheldon and I would run into her room to find her propped up in her crib, with both arms stretched out, stopping traffic in all directions.

With her eyes closed, and her face scrunched up in deep distress, she'd lament, "Just... just go... Just... just leave me... leave me NOW." It was like watching a scene between Brooke and Ridge from the soap opera "The Bold and the Beautiful," except the protagonist was wearing a diaper.

At other times, Allegra would add a dramatic breakfast order at the end. "Just go away..." *(long, serious pause)* "And go cook my eggs."

Allegra liked to be unique.

Forget your standard "Good morning." When she was barely able to talk, she'd surprise me with, "Bonjour." At one point, she swapped "Mommy" with "Mother," complete with an English accent, like she had stepped back into the 18th century. "Can I have a drink, Mother?" A week before leaving for America, she swapped it again for an American accent.

In later years, when I'd ask if she had finished on the toilet, she would respond with the French word "Fin," usually incorporated by filmmakers at the end of their films. And just to teach me a lesson or two, she'd elaborate, "'Fin' is for finished, Mommy."

Allegra felt she had rights equal to or above us. At 22 months, often after placing our order with the waitress at our favorite Japanese restaurant, Allegra would interrupt the waitress. "And I'll have the Miso soup and a smoothie. Thanks!" complete with a wink from her high chair.

And I'll have the Miso soup and a smoothie. Thanks!

Afterwards, I'd be tempted to eat her chubby legs. So I'd grab her, saying "I'm going to eat your fatty legs."

She'd respond peculiarly, laying down her rules. "Okay. Just don't use my stop sticks." That was her version of "chop sticks."

The Performer

Allegra was a star performer. As a teeny toddler, she loved acting out animals and had the entire zoo down pat.

I would ask, "What does the cow say?"

"Moo."

"What does the duck say?"

"Quack."

I must have had the flu when I taught her the zebra, because whenever we asked, "What would the zebra say?" she'd respond, "Cough, cough."

She also performed illnesses well. There were two incidents where we thought she was dying.

The first time, we rushed her to the emergency room, explaining, "Doctor, she's really, really ill."

He glanced at Allegra entertaining his staff, running around, roaring with laughter. We left with some prescribed medicine – one ice-block and some bubbles. She pretty much came home with a party bag.

The second time, we lined up in the crowded emergency room of the Children's Hospital at midnight. Allegra made the swift change from near-death to toddler nightclubbing.

The nurse looked at me, pointing to the others. "Do you see all the other kids here?"

I scanned the room full of seriously ill children, and then glanced at my disco-dancing showgirl. "Yes, ma'am."

"That's what sick children look like."

My mother and I went home a little embarrassed.

Other times, we had a live soap opera occurring in our house. Allegra would storm into the room, beat her chest with her fists, and yell, "Nobody listens to me in this house anymore. NOBODY!"

Then there was the episode when Allegra was pregnant for about a week. I tucked her into bed and she insisted, "Don't close my sleeping bag, because the doctor needs to pull the baby out when it's born." If only I had a camera.

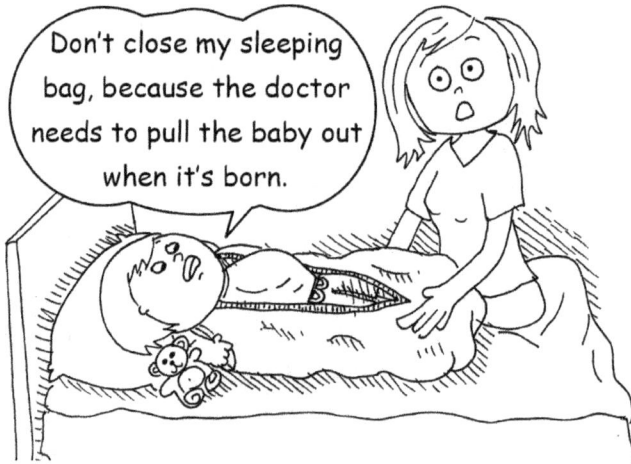

We even had tense confrontations with Allegra. Sometimes she'd look us in the eye and pensively declare, "Don't get angry at me and I won't get angry at you." What an ultimatum! As long as I didn't get angry, no one would get hurt.

She was definitely all about getting her way. Once, I was driving a long distance to my in-laws' when Allegra realized she left her toy boats behind and began screaming.

"Turn the car around now!"

"No. We have already driven a long way, and we are stuck in traffic."

Somewhat insulted by my remark, Allegra pronounced every consonant in detail, "No. We are not stuck. There's a space over there. You can turn around NOW." She pointed to a tiny gap on my right.

Great. I had a two-year-old backseat driver. I stuck to my guns and never turned around. Mommy won this time.

If there was an opportunity to be cheeky, she had to take it. One time, we were in a busy shopping center near Centrepoint in Sydney. I thought I had her under control, washing her hands in the ladies' room, when she suddenly bolted into the men's room to play hide-and-seek. I stood by the entrance, catching a glimpse of her hot pink leggings under a men's stall door.

"Allegra!" I wailed. "ALLEGRA!"

She thought it was hilarious, giggling behind the stall. Finally, my husband turned up and she ran out. Good grief.

Another time, she disappeared in the middle of a busy buffet restaurant. Sheldon used his special Allegra-vision and saw a long table of senior citizens shuffling. He headed for the table and found her weaving between their legs under the table.

"What are you doing here? You don't even know these people."

Allegra looked stunned herself, and she stared blankly at the elderly.

I considered getting her a toddler leash, since my friends had them for their kids. Friends debated whether that was mean or not. I personally thought it was good for her own safety – and for the safety of the elderly.

Our friend's cheeky two-and-a-half-year-old wore one for a wedding. We watched as she handed the handle of the leash to Allegra. Everyone in the room gasped, "Do you really want Allegra to lead you?" Allegra took the leash and led the way. That was double trouble.

These little spectacles were tolerable. It was the full-blown dramas that often left us shocked, speechless, or pointing fingers at each other. "She's your child."

The first was the water incident.

The Great Tanty

At thirteen months of age, Allegra sat, trying to drink a cup of water during a family celebration. As she was having slight difficulty, I cautiously assisted her, ever so gently supporting the cup, and then retreating quickly as you would do when feeding a lion.

I must have disrupted the delicate balance of her little ecosystem because she exploded into an ear-shattering rage. There was a full hour of screaming, spitting, angst, passion, kicking, and drama over her little cup of water – enough to win an Academy Award. Yikes! Even my parents were running for cover. I obviously shouldn't have gone too close to the lion. It was officially my first experience of a tanty – or great tantrum.

Tantrums came complimentary with the diva package. In fact, you even got a jumbo-sized helping. Some parents were fortunate enough to get the subdued variety in their welcome pack. Either way, tantrums were part of the pay-it-back scheme devised by a genius universal creator that decided to give us a taste of what we put our parents through.

Allegra's tantrums varied in shape and form. She often graced us with her personal favorites:

The Starfish: Allegra would lie face-down on the ground, screaming, with arms and legs stretched out, like a starfish. She liked giving it a twist by conveniently performing the Starfish in parking lots or public roads, as cars drove by.

The Karate Kid: This usually occurred when Allegra resisted leaving toy shops or coin-operated rides. I'd resort to picking her up, and she'd react with black belt karate kicks.

Cold Spaghetti: This was usually the same situation as above; however, she'd react by becoming weak and slippery like spaghetti, so that I couldn't pick her up.

The Stop Dance: The Stop Dance was a traveling tantrum that mostly occurred in shopping center aisles. Allegra would perform her drama on the floor and, as I'd walk away, she would momentarily stop, pick herself up, and follow me to the next aisle. Then she'd resume by throwing herself back on the floor as soon as my eyes glanced her way.

Once Allegra Stop Danced across all aisles of the supermarket and three tiers of the Westfield Shopping Center. I was so flustered that I called Sheldon. "Honey, I think we might have ourselves a diva."

He replied, "Woman, don't you know about online shopping?"

DANCE   STOP   DANCE

The Notebook: Sometimes, in protest, Allegra would burst into a slow motion, tear-jerking, emotional cry over something important like a wrinkle in her sock. It was like she'd watched the tear-jerking movie, "The Notebook." Allegra would finish her medley by returning to the earth, forming herself into a ball.

The Sandstorm: This was usually performed at a beach whenever Allegra was told the magic words, "It's time to go home." You get the picture.

The Edvard Munch: The Edvard Munch, or "silent scream," was my personal favorite. Allegra would scrunch her face in pain with mouth wide open, having such an intense cry that no sound came out.

The IFO (Invisible Flying Objects) and RFO (Real Flying Objects): Finally, there was the IFO. Allegra would get so angry she'd throw her arms at me like she was throwing invisible flying objects. Some parents are fortunate enough to experience Real Flying Objects, or RFO.

There are many more varieties that are worth studying, such as the Kanye (when a child storms a stage for not winning) and the spring roll (rolling on the ground). But for the purpose of this book, I have stuck to Allegra's best tantrums.

The Evacuation Process

Just as aircrafts carry a safety procedure booklet in case of an unexpected emergency, Sheldon and I followed an evacuation process. Failure to follow these steps could lead to grievous bodily harm or even fatality.

Step 1: Take ten steps backwards from the child.
Step 2: Act like the child is not yours. Expect strangers to ask the child, "Did you lose your mommy and daddy?"

Once Allegra ran out of steam, it all usually went well. For more tips on handling tantrums, please refer to Part II of this book, "Parents' Survival Kit."

Caught in the Firing Line

Unfortunately, beloved friends and family have been caught in a tantrum firing line, sustaining injuries.

Once, my sister kindly offered to babysit so we could attend a wedding. Sheldon and I were having a fabulous time, but decided to fulfill our parental duty by calling to check on Allegra. "How is she?"

My usually calm sister responded anxiously, "She's doing the Starfish! The Starfish! I have sweat coming out of my pores!"

We picked up Allegra and listened to my haggard sister recount the trauma. To this day, she still has Starfish flashbacks that terrorize her. She disappeared for a long time, rehabilitating herself until she finally had the courage to babysit again two years later.

My brother followed a similar pattern. He used to visit me daily, but stopped after one of her tanties.

"See you later. Um, I might not see you again for a couple of months."

I really believe during those times, Allegra became a natural contraceptive for my siblings. They took a big detour from having children.

Another time, we had the great "Panadol" incident. She had such a high temperature that we were told by the doctor to give her Panadol, a type of paracetamol. She absolutely refused that night, performing a mega combo three-hour tantrum. It was a combination of the Karate Kid, The Notebook, Cold Spaghetti and the Edvard Munch. My mother-in-law got the brunt of it, so I called my mother for reinforcement.

"Calm down, Anna. You know it can be the slightest thing that can make her turn around. Just go through everything."

So I began with the zoo animals.

"Take this medicine for the cow?"

"No."

"Do it for the frog?"

"No."

"The duck?"

"No."

I patiently listed every animal I could think of for over an hour. Finally, "Do it for the dolphin?"

"Okay."

She was so nonchalant about it. The dolphin had appeased her, so she swallowed and blissfully slept.

That was the thing. Allegra's tantrums were like tornados that ferociously exploded from nowhere, and soon disappeared into nothing at her slightest command.

The next day, Allegra had the boldness to tell me, "Don't be so dramatic, Mommy."

Work – my new holiday

The home visiting counselor saw my weariness and suggested I place Allegra into day care. I did need some distance from her, and I knew she'd benefit from social interaction.

I heard stories from other mothers about the guilt they felt parting with their children, so something must have been wrong with me because the thought of parting with Allegra was bliss.

I dropped her at day care when she was barely able to walk, and left that day feeling like I could actually breathe again.

The effects were immediate. Anxiety reduced, fear of the ticking tantrum time bomb gone – day care would have to deal with that. For the first time, I felt like myself again.

I applied for a part-time job in a photography studio. They asked me why I wanted the position and I answered bluntly, "I want a break from my daughter."

They were worried I'd be bored with the job, seeing that it didn't require much social interaction. I assured them, "Compared to all the screaming and tantrums at home, this would be heaven."

I started immediately.

The lady I was replacing showed me the computer and said, "I will take my three-year-old off my desktop background so you can put your daughter up."

I said, "No, thanks. I want an Allegra-free zone."

I know I sounded unloving, especially when mothers shed tears returning to work. I found the tantrums overbearing and enjoyed the chance to be on my own for just a few days a week. I eventually trained as a life coach and started my own business. It felt great to reclaim a part of my life by doing something I enjoyed. I now understood when teachers at work would say, "Work is my holiday."

Meanwhile, day care loved her. She was so interesting. She was such a diva, complete with finger-pointing, hands on the hips, and nuances in her voice. She'd crack up at other children's tantrums, probably because their poor attempts didn't compare with her expertise.

One day care teacher confronted me. "She is so dramatic that my friends don't believe the stories and want to meet her for proof."

Even my friends would tell me, "She must be learning all her diva-ness at day care."

I'd respond, "Unfortunately, I think it's the other way around. I think she is passing her knowledge to the other children."

Passing on her diva wisdom

How did I know Allegra was passing on her pearls of diva wisdom to other children? Their parents would tell me.

One time, a little girl pronounced an outlandish diva comment. Her mother exclaimed, "Where on earth did you learn that?"

She answered with one simple word. "Allegra."

Allegra also brainwashed younger children to worship her. Parents would tell me about their children singing "Happy Birthday" to Allegra when it wasn't Allegra's birthday. They'd even sing it in front of their own birthday cakes.

Allegra always had to be different. I would check the sleeping chart when I'd collect her. Under all the children's names it would say "Sleep." Under Allegra's name it would say "Rest."

I'd look over to the day care worker and she'd confirm, "Yep, she fake-slept again."

She had a tendency to pretend to sleep as they pat her painstakingly for an hour. Finally they would ask, "Allegra are you sleeping?" With her eyes closed, she would nod in reply.

Allegra always had to be different. She even claimed she was born in another country. At age two, before she had traveled to the East Coast of America, Allegra made the public declaration in front of her fellow day care buddies.

They were seated in a circle, celebrating Harmony Day. Harmony Day is a day when Australians celebrate cultural diversity. To acknowledge the different nations of the world, the manager asked each child, "Which country do you come from?"

Different children acknowledged their roots. Italy, Lebanon, India.

Of course, Allegra confidently responded, "New York."

"Don't you come from the Philippines and Australia?"

She was adamant. "No. I come from New York."

I always knew she was born on Broadway.

The Fire Starter

Nothing could ever compare to Allegra's biggest drama of all: The epic "Fire Drill."

One day, I innocently arrived at day care to pick up Allegra. The manager looked at me seriously.

"I need to talk to you about your daughter."

I half-covered my eyes with my hands, a little afraid to look. "Go, ahead. Tell me."

"Today we had the worst fire drill in the history of the day care because of your daughter."

I cleared my throat. "Uh-huh."

"Usually our fire drills are very organized. Allegra has done them before. I don't know why she reacted this way. I told the children, 'This is only pretend. These are the steps you need to follow.'"

I nodded, still hiding.

"When I said, 'Children it's time for the fire drill' Allegra threw her sandpit tools in the air and started screaming 'FIRE! FIRE! Don't even put on your shoes. They are just going to BURN! Everything is burning!' She was melodramatic. It sent the entire group of thirty children into hysterics."

"Oh, dear!"

"All the teachers couldn't control the children. They were running around, screaming. Allegra even tried to climb the fence. We finally went outside and she was still screaming, 'Fire' in the street. It was not a laughing matter at the time."

I didn't know whether to laugh or cry. I phoned Sheldon and my mother immediately.

My mother was laughing so much that she phoned back minutes later, "Can you tell me the story again? Do you have time?"

Friends were passing the story on to friends. People were commenting, "If Allegra wants a dramatic fire drill, she will get a dramatic fire drill," and "Just drop her off in Hollywood. I'll organize an agent."

Fortunately, the next day, Allegra gave me some good news. "Mommy, today I did not say, 'Fire.'"

"Good girl."

I knew one thing for certain. Allegra was not a neutral little girl. She would either create great havoc in this world, or great success.

I'm hoping for success.

Chapter 12

The Poo Chronicles

Everybody has their stories growing up; stories that are nostalgically shared years later at a close family gathering.

For me, it was my first perm when I was eight, during a trip to the Philippines. The hairdresser trimmed my bouffant in a circle so I looked like a circular garden hedge. I posed like Christie Brinkley in the photos, so I must have been proud of it.

For my brother, it was the first time he got his ears pierced in high school. He managed to hide it from our parents by wearing a pair of Yoda ears around the house for two weeks, pretending it was a dare. They caught him and sent him to Maliwat prison because they thought no employer would respectfully hire him.

As for Allegra, she will forever be renowned for her "Poo Chronicles."

We finally reached the stage of Allegra's life that I was not entirely looking forward to – potty training. The thought of spills all over the house and cleaning major accidents made me queasy. Would she cooperate? Would she play some form of hunger games? Would she give us an easy transition? Who was I kidding? Of course, Allegra would never settle for that. She made sure every little milestone was mixed with a bit of her spark. These thoughts raced through my mind, with the added pressure from my mother, emphasizing that we were all potty-trained by eighteen months.

The possessed potty

To appease the queen, we purchased a full-blown pink princess potty that played music when directly hit. Using our professional finger-pointing system, we thoroughly explained its basic function. "Pee-pee... potty. Poo-poo... potty."

She had better ideas for its use. It was a high-tech storage system. I'd open the potty to find toys, an orange, other fruit, pencils, and Sheldon's electric toothbrush squashed inside the tray. Lucky for him, she was peeing on the floor.

We followed suggestions by friends to leave the potty in the living room so she could access it easily. She finally understood it wasn't a storage system at all – it was her gold-class movie recliner! She'd watch entire Disney movies back to back with her pants down, lying on her potty as though it were a day bed. In the end, she'd have butt marks deeply grooved from the potty seat.

I really didn't like the fact that our meals were being served a metre away from her potty day bed, so I moved it back into the bathroom. It was there that the paranormal activity began. In the middle of the night while we were sleeping, the potty would suddenly play music. I'd get up and shudder to find Allegra sleeping soundly.

Other times, I'd hear an eerie noise so I'd fumble through the dark, imagining an intruder had arrived. The music would abruptly play and scare the living daylights out of me.

The potty was possessed by some potty-training toddler spirit. If

only that spirit would teach my daughter a thing or two.

It was time for some Ghostbuster extermination. "Pass me the screwdriver. We're getting those batteries out."

Hit and miss

Allegra was hit-and-miss with the potty. Perhaps she didn't understand us. The worst period was when she started hosting poo-poo tea parties. I know this sounds disgusting, but it's a normal bodily function. If you have children, you should be immune to it.

Allegra often played with tea sets in the shower. I think she truly had no control over her little bottom. She'd be crouched over, preparing her tea set, and voila. She'd deposit her surprise.

To my horror, I'd ask "Allegra, why?"

As soon as she'd discover what had happened, she'd hysterically scream, wanting to escape the shower like it was extra-terrestrial. She did this a couple of times, even at my in-laws' house. Once, she even made a neat deposit directly on the toy dinner plate. The poor thing was in a frenzy, scared of her own serving. My cousin simply ran away, grossed out.

Poor me. I had to work out what to do with it.

I was told by friends, "Take the diaper off, because children don't like the feeling of poo in their pants."

Allegra was the opposite. I think she rather enjoyed it. She would do it silently in her pants and not tell anyone. The stench would give her away and our negotiations would begin.

"Allegra, why didn't you tell me? Let's change your diaper."

She would hush me with her hands, whispering, "Shhhh. Just leave it. My poo is sleeping."

She learned about the germs from a show called Yo Gabba Gab-

Allegra, let's change your diaper.

Shhhh. Just leave it. My poo is sleeping.

Another time, after silently pooping in her pants, she protested against being changed. I tried to reason with her. "If you don't let me change you, you are going to get all these ugly germs that will make you sick."

ba, so I hoped my words carried some weight. The cheeky monkey twisted it around to her advantage. "Well, then. If I get sick, I will just go to the doctor and I'll get a jelly bean."

Another time, I caught her hiding in her room. "What are you doing, Allegra?"

"Nothing," she responded, poking her finger at her bottom. "Don't worry. I'm pushing it back in. I'm pushing it back in."

Public displays

Allegra had a knack for choosing the most inconvenient public spots to drop her number twos. Sometimes, when we'd wait to see her favorite Indian doctor, she'd yell out something embarrassing.

"I'm here to see the black doctor."

She did this once with my sister, who cringed in the public place. "I'm so embarrassed by the child's somewhat racist remark."

On this particular day, the waiting room was packed full of people. A new female doctor walked into the room and called out, "Allegra Garcia?"

With precision timing, Allegra looked up and announced in a megaphone voice, "But I'm doing a POO!"

People burst out laughing. They watched as I grabbed Allegra's hand, trying to force her to move toward the doctor. Instead, she refused, remaining stationed at her spot.

"Let me finish my poo."

So the doctor stood there waiting until Allegra was all done, in front of the audience. I was completely embarrassed.

When Allegra returned the following week, she repeated the same procedure, you know, for old time's sake.

Thank goodness a day care teacher, Mary, paved the way for me.

"Do you want me to toilet train her at day care? I'm training the entire group so it should make it easier. They copy each other."

That was my golden ticket. I almost did a happy dance.

That day care teacher spent every twenty minutes taking a group of two- to three-year-old children to the toilet. Sometimes she'd spend 90% of her day there. I didn't know how she did it.

And so began the dramatic day care poo stories.

Day care poo dramas

Every time I collected Allegra from day care, I braced myself for some dramatic story. However, I was not prepared for an entire year of stories with a poo twist. It could have made a good DVD Box Collection: Season One, Season Two, and Season Three. The first one was something I would never forget.

I arrived, as usual, to day care to pick up Allegra. I sensed something interesting had happened when Mary turned to Allegra and said, "Do you want to tell Mommy what happened today?"

Expecting some happy news, I looked wide-eyed at Allegra.

She nonchalantly answered, "I pooed in the cubby house."

I reacted just as any parent would after hearing such joyful news. I froze.

Mary explained the scenario to me. The children were playing outdoors in the playground. As usual, one of the teachers announced, "Children, it's time to go to the bathroom."

In a matter-of-fact way, Allegra responded, "But I already went."

The teacher was surprised. "Where?"

Allegra pointed to the cubby house. "Over there."

On closer inspection, they discovered Allegra had walked into the outdoor cubby house, dropped her pants, completed a number two, and then resumed playing in the playground.

To make it more interesting, another child had walked in and stepped on Allegra's work. Then another kid vomited in reaction to the scene. Finally, all the children had gathered around the scene of the crime. They were fascinated.

"It was their excitement of the day," Mary concluded.

In the midst of my disbelief, a four-year-old girl excitedly ran into the room, giving me a vital piece of the story. "It was this big." She formed a circle with her little hands as her eyes twinkled.

"They really do get excited."

To conclude, one of the saintly teachers cleaned Allegra, the cubby house, and the other child.

Sheldon simply responded, "You better get the day care teachers a really good present for Christmas."

Allegra liked to spread her work around. During another episode, she decided to drop her pants and do her business in the middle of the indoor playroom, surrounded by kids. The children watched in awe as Allegra hastened them away, guarding her territory.

"Stay back! Stay away! It's disgusting! It's disgusting." With her free hand, she picked up the toy phone to call Sheldon and tell him about it. "Daddy, I pooed at day care. It's disgusting."

Other days, I'd pick up Allegra and ask her my usual question while driving home. "How was day care, baby?"

I'd expect, "I did drawing" or "We did some cooking."

Instead, she'd respond casually, "I pooed in my Nikes."

One day, Allegra scared me when I asked her, "How was day care baby?"

"I pooed in the sandpit."

I looked at the teacher, who dismissed the claim. "No, she didn't."

I went home relieved, yet wondered why she would say such a thing.

The next day, the prophecy came true. "She pooed in the sandpit," the day care teacher confirmed.

I couldn't believe it was premeditated.

All Sheldon could say was, "I'm so proud of our little achiever. She sets a goal, and then she goes out and achieves it."

The teachers told me there were times when dealing with Allegra was like a scene from a medical drama. Just as nurses used scissors to cut patients' clothing off in emergencies, the day care teachers used scissors to remove Allegra's poo-filled clothing. Lovely, I know.

It got to the point where I would no longer question if she did a poo at day care. Instead, I wondered where she did it this time. Every day I'd collect my special package, clothing wrapped in a plastic. I'd stand in the laundry room with my eyes and nose shut, trying to wash her clothing and shoes, reaffirming to myself, "I love motherhood. I love it."

I began posting her stories on Facebook. Sometimes I felt like I belonged to another universe. I read posts from other parents talking about how angelic and thoughtful their children were. One person commended the parent saying, "Good children are a reflection of their parents."

I thought about Allegra and her poo dramas. If that was the case, what did this say about us? Were we poopy parents? I even had a friend tell me, "Anna, I have friends who tell such loving stories on Facebook, and then I have you."

Was that a good thing or a bad thing?

By her third birthday, I questioned if I'd ever get her toilet trained. I read books that promised easy transitions within three days. They didn't work with her.

We even used her birthday presents as bait to lure her to the toilet. "One present can be opened per poo-poo in the toilet."

It took her a month to get the Barbie.

My friend eventually told me, "Don't force her. We tried with our twins and they just couldn't understand. A few months later, they did it by themselves. A chemical releases inside them that tells them they're ready."

So I finally gave up, letting Allegra be. While we traveled overseas, that chemical was released. She miraculously decided it was time. After 457 days of trying, Allegra was finally toilet trained.

Our poo girl extraordinaire finally graduated. It was a cause for celebration.

Chapter 13

Citizens of Hawaii

There's nothing like the joys of traveling.

Plenty of sunshine and relaxation, freedom from repetitive rituals at work, and the sheer excitement of exploring a new culture. Of course, I was referring to traveling in the pre- Allegra days. After Allegra was born, traveling was reduced to any form of transport, including a trip to the local gas station.

Seeing the world was what I loved the most. So I grieved deeply when I thought about waiting until Allegra's wedding day before we could take off. There were reasons Sheldon and I believed traveling would be difficult:

1. Financial – Dropping to one income made it difficult.
2. Getting leave from a workaholic firm was nearly as impossible as getting Allegra to sleep. Sheldon hadn't even passed his probation yet.
3. Allegra was so unsettled.
4. The amount of baby baggage would be like moving house.
5. Even if we did get the chance, we wouldn't enjoy it because our stress-ometer would be off the charts.
6. She would scream in the plane.
7. She would scream in the plane.
8. She would scream in the plane.

Any benefits of traveling (a clear mind, relaxation, seeing sights) would simply be countered by the child we traveled with (an unsettled baby, listening to a stress-inducing scream that caused paralysis).

Consequently, I resigned to watching planes pass over me as I hung the laundry. I accepted fate, that planes would forever be two inches in length, belonging to the unreachable sky.

Fight-or-flight

After moving back home from my in-laws' house, Allegra's screaming sessions and hunger games had peaked. Without my in-laws to help, I was either crying on the phone with my girlfriend or simply crumbling. But I noticed something happens in the midst of adversity. You muster all your strength to find a way through the impossible. The fight-or-flight response activated within me, so I turned to Sheldon and smoothly said, "I'm getting her a passport."

I obviously chose flight, literally. I needed to get away. I needed a sanity holiday. Besides, why did traveling have to stop because of a tiny baby? I didn't care if it meant staying in the cheapest hotel, being on a tight budget, and not being able to do much activity. I was going to make this happen.

I felt the glimmer return to my eyes as I searched for whatever savings were hidden away in secret crevices. I organized Allegra's passport and I told myself, "I'm booking the first holiday deal that pops up on TV."

The Universe must have heard me because immediately an extremely cheap deal to Hawaii magically showed up on television. It was perfect.

"You want to travel with that baby?" Sheldon clearly didn't share my enthusiasm. "Are you crazy? She's going to be screaming on the plane the entire time. Can't you pick a location that's closer, like 30 minutes away from home? How will I get time off?"

I knew it would be stressful, but once we crossed the most challenging part, there was the prize on the other side – beautiful Hawaii. We could also catch up with my cousin and friends living there.

"I'll find a way to keep her quiet on the plane. I promise." That was like saying, "Pigs might fly," but it helped me to close the deal.

After Sheldon disgruntledly agreed, I did my happy Hawaiian dance.

There was one more thing to do; notify the queen of travel and pleasure herself, my sister. She was gallivanting around the world after visiting Santa's home in the North Pole.

I sent my text message and she replied with four simple words, "Book me a ticket."

Could this day get any better? We just scored ourselves a free babysitter.

She added, "Cancel your accommodation; I'm upgrading us to an apartment."

I couldn't believe our fortune. We now had a fairy-travel-mother so we could finally go to the ball.

In-flight remedies

I still had something major to combat – how to travel with a screaming nine-month-old during a night flight? She wasn't any nine month old; she was Allegra.

There had to be a solution. I searched online, gathered tips from friends and doctors, and began probing every chemist for baby-friendly remedies that helped them settle or relax. Some remedies warned the opposite effect, making 10% of babies more alert. We tested this out. Why did we have to be the lucky 10%?

Finally, Sheldon purchased a natural remedy that you sprayed on the infant's tongue when he or she was distressed. I kept it in my pocket like a Taser.

A turbulent flight

We arrived at the airport, certain we had enough reinforcement to get us through.

"Mrs. Garcia, the flight is absolutely full. These are the remaining seats left."

The seats we pre-booked were reallocated. Instead, Sheldon, Allegra, the baby bag, and I were squashed between two grown muscle-men in two seats. It was like a body-building sandwich and we were the filling. It wasn't easy to get out and climb over the sleeping giants, so we remained stationed, barely able to move. My sister was safely tucked away in another section, enjoying her Allegra-free sanctuary.

The flight took off, dinner was served, and the lights were dimmed. My eyes scanned the aircraft. People were spreading their blankets and adjusting their pillows, so my heart began racing. Allegra, please don't... please don't start.

"WAAAAAAAAAAAAAAAAAH."

We frantically tried moving her in and out of the baby seat, but she screamed even louder.

I looked at the people shuffling around me, offering my sweet apologetic face. "I'm sorry. I'm sorry."

When that didn't work, I tried my victim it's-not-my-fault face. There were other babies on the flight, but they were only murmuring or sleeping soundly.

We tried the rescue remedy.

"It's not working!" I whispered. I lay her up and down and turned her all around, doing the hokey pokey in my seat.

Back at home, whenever Allegra was unsettled, I had the luxury to walk around the room and take my time. Here on the plane, I had around half an inch of space to move or rock her, and I needed a harness to climb over the sleeping giants. The clock was ticking, counting down the seconds I had left before being shot with death stares. Tick... tick... tick.

The seatbelt signal lit up. "This is your captain speaking. We are experiencing some slight turbulence."

I was waiting for him to add, "Her name is Allegra, so please return to your seats and fasten your seatbelts."

155

I equipped myself with a comeback, in case I got the death stare. You passengers paid for economy seats, so don't expect a first-class sleep.

After some acrobatic work, we managed to reduce her outbursts to every five to ten minutes. This was as long as I held her in the most uncomfortable Pilates position for the next – well, six hours.

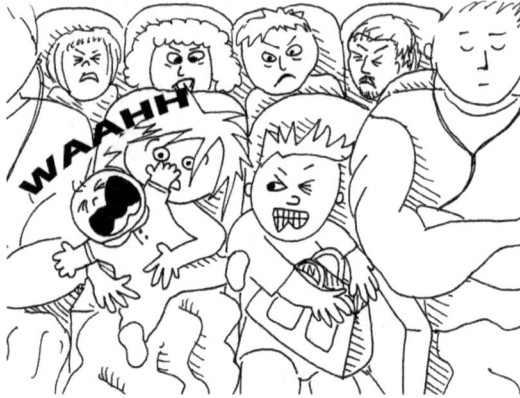

At some point, flying over the Pacific Ocean, Sheldon nudged me. "Pass me that baby rescue spray."

He didn't spray it on Allegra. He opened his mouth and sprayed it on his tongue. We were the ones needing rescuing. So I took some spray myself. It was the worst flight ever in our lives.

When we arrived in beautiful Honolulu, Sheldon said to me, fuming, "I don't care if we have to become citizens of Hawaii, I am not taking a flight back with THAT baby."

I reckon he would have divorced me on the spot, if he had the energy to sign the documents.

I didn't know what he was grouchy about. I was the one with numb limbs from my back-breaking Pilate position. It took a couple of days for him to unwind. Thanks to my sister being an extra hand, we had the most amazing time.

There were several highlights from that trip. One was snorkeling with Sheldon at Hanouma bay. I could feel myself healing from anxiety as I watched the giant turtles feeding off coral a few feet away from us. We also did the other most exciting activity on the island – a field trip to Costco, thanks to our friends Jason and Rowena.

Before Costco landed in Sydney, we had heard great legends about the mega warehouse and the special secret club entry. We finally stood in awe at the mammoth monument, observing everything like a museum, without purchasing due to luggage restrictions. The jumbo-sized portions were like rare artifacts belonging to civilizations that owned giant pantries.

I picked up a box and excitedly yelled down the aisle, "Sheldon, this one makes pancakes for 150 people!"

Half-annoyed, he snapped back, "Why would you make pancakes for 150 people? Put that back!"

He did, however, allow me to take a brownie mix home, fit for 100 people. That fifteen-pound box was my Costco souvenir.

But nothing could beat the highlight that converted the very grouchy Sheldon into a relaxed tourist. No, it wasn't the beautiful scenery, the circle island tour, or the luau. It was American television, in all its reality TV and infomercial glory.

I watched him exclaim from the couch, "Anna, I think we need one of those. It chops, blends, juices, and cleans all at the same time. Unbelievable!"

Departing at the airport, I discovered a $50 US bill left over. I said to Sheldon, "This must be a sign we need to return. What do you say if we trekked across America with Allegra?"

It sounded ridiculous at the time, but I held it close to my heart and it came to be, two and a half years later.

The New Law

When we returned home, Sheldon and I declared a new law. Every year, no matter how big or small, we would take time to travel on a short vacation. It didn't mean it was easy, but we were willing to find a way to make it happen and to bear the plane trips.

We traveled to Fiji when she was eighteen months. We almost canceled the trip because of Allegra's ear infection, which four sets of antibiotics could not cure. After praying like crazy, she was miraculously cured the day before leaving. Even the doctor was shocked.

We also took small trips interstate with my family. One particular trip was to the Sunshine Coast, in Queensland, with my parents.

To my delight, the lady at the airport terminal said, "Unfortunately, you are in a separate seat from your husband and daughter."

That was a bonus. I thoroughly enjoyed the hour flight, fully capitalizing on the rare opportunity to watch movies and chill out. The flight was, unfortunately, too short.

Sheldon had the opposite experience. When we arrived, he gasped, "That was the longest flight ever. And why do I always get stuck with Allegra?"

On our flight back, I wasn't so lucky. We were, once again, separated when a kind stewardess noticed and made efforts to reunite us.

"Sir, do you mind swapping seats so we can keep this family together?"

I begged her, "Really, I'm fine where I am."

Sheldon, on the other hand, said, "Please move my wife next to her child."

When we arrived at the Sunshine Coast, my mother got a first-hand opportunity to mind Allegra over five consecutive days.

For years, my mother kept hounding me, believing Allegra was a by-product of my weak parenting skills.

"Stop spoiling Allegra."

"You need to show her who's boss."

"I had you doing chores by age three."

"You were nothing like Allegra. You were behaved."

My mother was a believer of "tough love." She introduced Allegra to "tough luck" time, which was specific time dedicated to not getting her own way. She believed she could transform Allegra in less than a week, so she sent Sheldon and me away to enjoy a swim.

When we returned, we were surprised to find Allegra riding my parents like a donkey.

My mother pleaded, "She made us do it. Ouch, my back! I swear we had no say."

So much for her taking control.

Allegra and business don't mix

Another time, Sheldon took a business trip interstate to Melbourne when Allegra was extremely difficult.

As Allegra's meltdowns were affecting me, I pleaded with Sheldon, "Please don't go. Don't leave me alone with her."

I can't believe he actually told his boss, "My wife doesn't want me to go because she can't handle our daughter."

Within an hour, I got a call and was told to pack my bags and Allegra's things. His boss added us to Sheldon's luggage.

I thought a one-hour flight wouldn't be so bad. But, as we boarded a plane full of business men and women in suits with briefcases, we could literally hear the sighs of despair as they watched Allegra board.

She screamed like she owned the plane. Embarrassed, we just prayed for the hour flight to be over.

Despite my battles with her, I actually loved being in Melbourne because it was the first time ever that Allegra was happy to sit in the stroller for more than five minutes without shouting. That meant I could actually sight-see.

Sheldon wasn't so happy. I think we ruined his time there. He was triple-stressed, working until midnight, and then dealing with our screaming drama girl.

We've never been invited on a business trip again.

The big adventure

The big adventure occurred when Allegra was three years old. We decided it was time to meet her favorite stars – the Disney gang.

I prepared Allegra by asking, "Would you like to fly on a plane again?"

She answered, "No, because it's too high and I might fall out."

We booked six stops across America and revisited our homeland, Hawaii.

There were so many obstacles working against us. Sheldon had never taken more than 11 days off a year for the past ten years because he always had deadlines. The cost quoted to me by an agent was well over $20,000. How would we get time off? And Allegra was testing us with her tantrums. Sheldon and I would probably kill each other if we didn't have a babysitter on the journey.

It was around this time that I started training as a life coach, and started learning about using dream boards, visualization, and using the law of attraction to achieve goals. Every day, I imagined myself in New York with the wind blowing through my hair as I sailed past the Statue of Liberty. I also visualized Hawaii, Florida, and Los Angeles. I kept focusing on my goal as if it had already happened.

Within a year, all of our plans unexpectedly fell into place. Sheldon was approved for four weeks off (that, in itself, was a miracle) and relatives offered to host us for parts of the trip. We got a free stopover in Hawaii and half-price plane tickets. My in-laws also joined us, so babysitting was covered and Sheldon and I no longer had to kill each other.

Even Sheldon remarked, "I can't believe how everything magically came together."

Good luck, America

So off we went and, fortunately, by then iPads had been invented to keep toddlers occupied. Allegra managed to have some major events occur within the first two days of the trip.

In Hawaii, she requested an orange-colored smoothie. When she saw the papaya was at least a shade or two off from the orange color she expected, she released an emotional, moving "The Notebook." The entire International Market place was watching. Even the birds stopped chirping.

The smoothie man was so entertained by her drama that he couldn't stop laughing, and offered a free fruit smoothie of her choice. Her emotional dramas did have benefits. We were scoring free food.

This was followed by an epic sandstorm tanty right in the heart of the busiest section of Waikiki beach. After telling Allegra it was time to leave, she began screaming, performing a fireworks display using sand. As usual, Sheldon and I did our evacuation process, taking ten steps back, camouflaging in the crowd like we didn't know her.

The spectacle was so moving that an American stranger yelled out loud to Allegra, "You must be a movie star. And ACTION!"

On cue, she screamed her little head off, whirling flying sand everywhere.

She eventually calmed down and, finally, hugged us with tears, saying, "I'm sorry."

The same man was so moved that he said, "Aw. I like how this movie ended."

Whenever we needed something that I had forgotten to pack, Allegra simply networked by the pool and managed to score it. Even the most obscure items. She'd strike up a conversation with the sun bathers and the swimming tourists, then somehow twist them into offering us goods. Allegra had some sort of black market operation

going with the tourists. We stocked up enough free pharmaceuticals that week that we could have opened a store.

I doubted her methods at first. One technique was to climb directly on the swimsuit-clad elderly people and to strike up a conversation.

I would intervene by saying, "Allegra, get off the lady's thighs." What else can you say when you see your daughter nestled in a stranger's cellulite? She did this to a few women. Luckily, they found it adorable.

With the younger generation, she would point her finger at a male and ask in an interrogatory manner, "Are you a girl?" Or she'd ask a female, "Are you a boy?"

She'd also ask the most inappropriate questions to strangers, like, "How old are you?" right in front of a big audience.

Allegra did this all over America with shop assistants, strangers on the street, and passengers on flights.

Waking up in Vegas

Stopping over in Las Vegas was exciting. We knew this would be an exhilarating experience the moment we saw slot machines in the airport.

Unfortunately, it wasn't "all that" to Allegra. The most excitement she displayed was the day she saw a vision through the glass at the Venetian Hotel. It was a beautiful bride celebrating her wedding day with a group of friends. Allegra did what any star-struck three-year-old does. She pressed her hands and face onto the glass in awe, doing a blow fish.

The princess bride noticed, came out, and crouched down to speak to her new fan. Allegra greeted her by coughing and spluttering all over the bride's face.

I said my usual, "I'm sorry, I'm sorry."

I'm sure her new husband was appreciative of Allegra's wedding gift – a nice little illness for their honeymoon.

It was in Las Vegas that Allegra also started modelling and dressing toddler-skanky. I'd try to place a T-shirt on her, and she'd reply, "Mommy, I want to wear my T-shirt like this – off the shoulder." Her accessory was a doll, given by her aunty Eileen, which she named "Vegas."

I said, "It's time to get you out of Sin City and turn you back into a little girl. Orlando, Florida, here we come."

Disney World – The scariest place on earth?

When most people think of Disney World, they anticipate the most magical kingdom on earth. I took for granted that Allegra, the biggest Disney fan of all, would go ballistic with Cinderella's castle and all the Disney characters.

Instead, it had the opposite effect on Allegra. She came home terrified. It was the catalyst for a series of nightmares.

Have you actually experienced the rides? With dark and scary attractions like "Snow White's Scary Adventures" and giant-sized sea villains from "The Little Mermaid," no wonder it was absolutely freaking scary for a three-year-old. Loud bangs and noises added to the horror as the carriages jolted through the different rooms in certain attractions.

Allegra even sat through a production of "Beauty and the Beast" with a hat covering her face.

She came home with an increased imagination, absolutely petrified of everything in her bedroom.

"Get it out. Get the scary monster out," she'd scream, turning the miniscule pattern in the wood grain of her dresser into a giant beast.

I suppose it didn't help that we put Allegra on scary rides like the Kali River Rapids at Disney's Animal Kingdom. Since she met the height restrictions, we innocently thought the river raft ride was gentle and easy going. For some reason, the heavy waves kept crashing on her, and I was completely dry. She didn't enjoy it one bit.

"Don't worry, baby. It's nearly over." I looked over my shoulder and saw the water path ending. "Uh-oh."

There was a huge, steep waterfall right behind Allegra. Even I found that scary. We accelerated down the 30-foot waterfall, and Allegra received the full impact of the water.

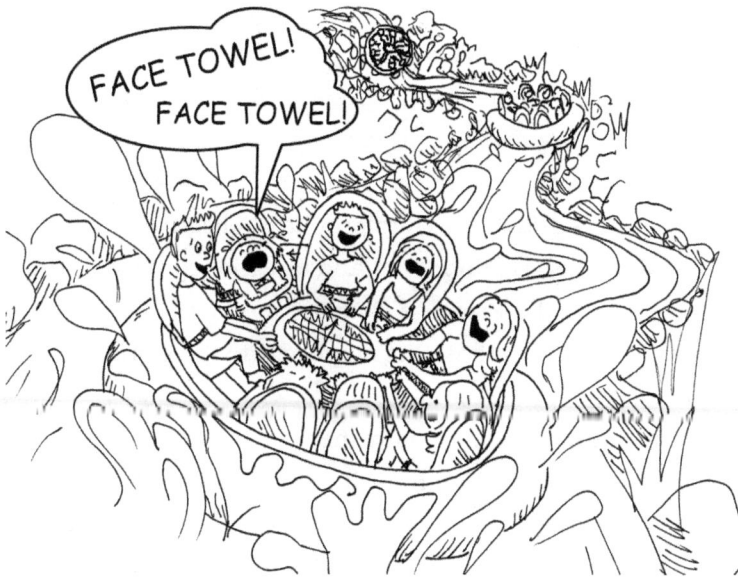

She screamed, "Face towel! FACE TOWEL!"

I think she had no desire to try anymore rides after that. From there onwards, she declared Disney World was the scariest place on earth. Fortunately, Cinderella saved the day.

Prom night

On our last evening, Allegra finally enjoyed a part of Disney World. It was the character dining experience that we booked with Cinderella and the cast.

Before the event started, my mother-in-law nudged me. "Are you going to get her a costume?"

With a closet full back at home, I wasn't going to buy another one. However, there was a little bit of peer group pressure going on. You see, Disney World was full of little four-foot princesses. They were a species of salon-pampered glitter girls, walking freely in the parks, all paid for by mommies and daddies around the world.

Literally, little girls could go into a Bibbity Bobbity Boo Salon and get the full do, hair, makeup, nails, and costume for about $200. You'd see these little Asian and African American girls coming out with blonde hair extensions and glitter sparkles in her hair.

The pressure was on. I succumbed to buying a basic princess dress. My mother-in-law offered to purchase Allegra's hair accessory. Like pageant agents, we pondered and questioned tiara vs. tiara for a gruelling hour in the Princess Couture store.

In the end, it was worth it. She stepped into the glorious ballroom glowing like it was prom night.

Her eyes lit up when she finally met her idol – Cinderella. I have to commend Disney World for having characters that looked identical to the animated films. I nearly jumped onto Captain Sparrow because he looked exactly like Johnny Depp. The Cinderella meeting was the best moment during our Disney World trip.

Allegra met Cinderella again 30 minutes later down the street.

"Mommy, why does Cinderella look different?"

"Um... She just fixed her hair differently." I wasn't going to explain how many Cinderella shifts there were across the entire park.

In the end, there was one very happy, starry-eyed girl that went home under the Disney magical spell. That was me. I LOVED Disney World, more than Allegra did.

"Allegra, let down your hair."

We finally arrived in New York, Allegra's apparent place of birth. She had been practicing singing "Empire State of Mind" by Alicia Keys for a couple of months, complete with a booty dance. So I thought she'd feel right at home in the city of Broadway dramas, fashion, and the arts.

On Top of the Rock, Allegra showed the people of Manhattan what she was made of, by performing her big debut.

"WAAAAAAAAAHHHHHHHHHHH!"

Her New York City greeting was a monumental "The Notebook" tantrum complete with a snotty noise. It was her twentieth Oscar-winning performance.

We couldn't remember what it was about. It probably had to do with me touching her hair. She dragged a long scarf all over New York, attaching one end permanently to her head, pretending to be Rapunzel. I guess the drama was due to her prince not turning up at the tower on time.

Allegra completed her tour of Manhattan with a visit to the Guggenheim museum. I believe Sheldon would have enjoyed the artworks if the guard hadn't kicked them out because of Allegra's disruption. Eventually, Sheldon settled for a more easy-going activity, suited to Allegra – ice cream in Central Park. She probably thought, "My plan worked."

Fortunately, all the hotels we had stayed in had two double beds in each room. I slept on my own, while Allegra slept next to Sheldon. One night, the tables were turned when I found Sheldon lying in my bed.

"What are you doing there?"

"Allegra kicked me out. She also told me to face the other way and look at the wall."

I was enjoying all that space to myself, so I said, "You can't stay here. Get back over to your bed."

He muttered something along the lines of, "I've just been kicked out twice by two women."

Our final stops were with family. They met Allegra and loved her for being "unusual." She also loved them.

When we returned, she kept telling me, "I love her. I love that aunty. I love her so much. Eh, what's her name?" If only she remembered the names of those people she loved so much. If she couldn't remember her loved ones, she often gave them a new name.

We do question whether the trip was worth taking at her age. Would she even remember? The day care teacher clarified this one for me.

Months later, while the day care teacher was talking about her friend vacationing across America to different states, Allegra added her two cents worth.

With a hand on her hip and a diva sigh, she smugly said, "Been there! Done that!"

The day care teacher apologized to her majesty. "Sorry, Allegra, if I haven't traveled as much as you have."

She just gave her that look as though she were saying, "Woman, you have got to get moving."

Allegra completed the epic American adventure by vomiting all over Sheldon's pants one hour into the fifteen-hour flight back to Sydney.

Traveling with Allegra was always an adventure and part of the memories I love the most. I realized there was no changing Allegra. She was ready to embark on the world, whether they liked it or not. Somewhere across the globe, between the splendor, drama, and airplane vomits, I could finally say the words, "I love you," and deeply mean it.

Chapter 14

Allegra Wears Prada

You know your child is a little bit high maintenance when:

1. There is a long gap of silence on the phone when you ask your mother to babysit.
2. Your mother responds after the long gap by saying, "Okay, I will sacrifice for you," because it is a sacrifice to spend time with her long-awaited, prized grandchild.
3. When your siblings lock their doors when you visit.
4. When your child knocks on the other side of a bedroom door after waking up to say, "I'm here," and your sister responds by telling you, "If you ignore the noise, it will go away."
5. When you hear a united sigh of relief from your family when you say your child is not sleeping over.
6. When your older brother bypasses visiting altogether when visiting from interstate.

In our case, Allegra was a bona fide, extra high maintenance, princess fashionista. They could have interchanged "The Devil" with "Allegra" and called the movie, "Allegra wears Prada."

I knew the name "Allegra" had links to high fashion. After all, Allegra Versace was the Italian heiress to Gianni Versace. In the movie "Hitch," the character Allegra was played by model Amber

Valetta, so some form of fashionista was bound to infiltrate her being. It all began at a very tender age.

The Beginning

I first noticed her natural flair for fashion when she was crawling. Allegra managed to dig out Sheldon's dirty underwear from the laundry basket, and wrap it around her head like a boho fashion headband.

You should have seen me flying through the air in slow motion trying to stop her. "NO!" I was too late. She was already admiring herself in the mirror. Ew.

When she started walking, she would collect all the handbags available and hook them onto any remaining limb she had available. She also managed to pull out my Victoria's Secret lace-trimmed underwear and twist it a couple of times over her body, weaving her arms in and out.

"What are you doing Allegra?" I couldn't really get mad. She constructed a rather sophisticated-looking bolero. *I probably could wear that. Should I sketch it?* I grabbed my camera, but it was too late.

I would always get suspicious when the house was quiet. "Allegra, why are you so quiet?"

Turning the corner, I'd find the toddler near the laundry basket trying on a bra as though she was saying, "I'm not sure about this color."

There were other interesting days as a toddler, when Allegra had bra meltdowns. I still remember the giant tantrums at breakfast over wanting to wear a bra to day care.

"I want a bra! WAAAHHHH!"

After a perturbed morning, I'd dig out her baby tropical bikini and tie it over her grey tracksuit.

The kids and teachers were impressed. "Wow, I like your outfit."

In true Allegra style, she'd take it all in, radiating like a goddess.

The Day Spa

When she was around two years old, she extended her fashion horizons. Move over, basic wardrobe. Allegra wanted the day spa experience. Thanks to her Aunty Charlotte, she was introduced to the world of nail polish, the sparkling array of glittering colors that absolutely belonged to Allegra's dazzling biosphere.

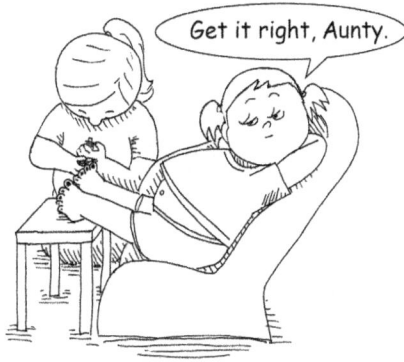

My original plan was to ban all nail polish and the color pink until she was at least sixteen. But that would be like fighting nature; fighting a tidal wave that was coming in my direction regardless of whether I approved. Her flair and desire for such scintillating things was simply innate. It was best just to ride out the wave.

Allegra watched attentively as her aunties pampered her with a manicure and pedicure. Like a professional, Allegra fanned her fingers out, blowing her nails to complete the process.

Pret-a-porte

I noticed her fussiness when it came to wearing her pret-a-porter or ready-to-wear collection. Since her clothing would simply be stained and torn at day care, I often slapped on a T-shirt and leggings.

With such distaste for my selection, Allegra would erupt in the middle of the neighborhood street, "This top is not cute! This top is NOT CUTE!"

It was true. What would Lagerfeld think?

Another time, I dared to put on her hooded top.

She revolted. "This top makes my HEART VOMIT!" and wailed for an hour. Of course, she chose to have a meltdown usually on the days I was late for work.

Her fussiness extended overseas. In San Francisco, Allegra stomped her feet in a store when I tried to place a jacket on her.

"This doesn't match my pants! This doesn't match my pants!"

We constantly used reverse psychology to curb her strong will. "Put on this jacket."

"NO!"

"Okay. It's my jacket then."

"No, it's mine!"

Fussiness even extended to her hair. One time, she had an ultra-pony-tail tantrum. I tried to tie it up as per her detailed request.

"Do it like this, Mommy."

So I tried.

"That's not the right way."

I tried again.

"That's not the right way. Do it like this. Like THIS!" She marked the exact position with her hands.

I tried again and again, until she had a monster meltdown.

"WAAAAAAAAH."

After the ninth time and many tears shed, I finally got it right. Between you and me, the final ponytail looked just like the first.

She was always aware of her looks. There was a stage in her early days when she went around day care saying, "I have blue eyes. I have long hair."

I'd look at her thinking, Y*ou have neither of those.*

The day care teacher asked me, "Why does she think that?"

I looked blankly – no idea! Allegra challenged me by tilting her head to the side in front of the mirror so that the length appeared longer than it actually was.

She later surprised me by becoming her very own hair stylist at age three. She simply walked into the room on a Sunday morning, having chopped the middle of her hair off with the nail scissors.

"Mommy I cutted my hair."

"Oh, dear."

She was nonchalant about it, so I asked, "Where did you put the rest of your hair?"

Unapologetic, Allegra took my hand and led me to her room, where she had picked up the hair and stuffed it under a lantern in the corner.

"Over there."

She was quite pleased with herself.

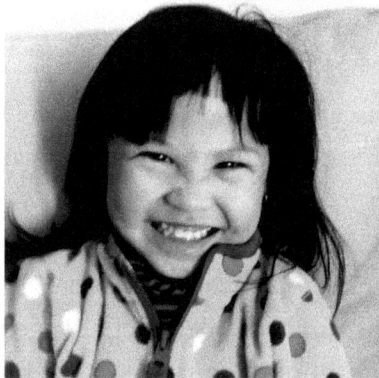

Allegra's designer haircut.

180

Thoughts raced through my mind. What am I going to do with this? Within minutes, I had successfully trimmed her bangs to a length one inch. It was the kind of bangs you gave your Barbie when you had that genius idea, as a kid, to become its hairdresser.

Anna Wintour

Allegra evolved into Anna Wintour. She became the fashion editor-in-chief of "Vogue" magazine, determining what was in season and what was not. Anything pink was in all year. Anything that passed the "flair" test was also in all year. For those ignorant about princess fashion, the flair test was the measure that a skirt rose during a 360-degree spin.

Allegra often cried, "I'm not a boy. I don't want to wear pants. I want to wear a dress."

When I'd place a dress on her, her crying would momentarily subside. But, after doing the spin test, she'd soon discover the dress had minimal lift, and the screaming would resume. So parents with their very own fashionistas roaming around the house, don't even *think* of getting a straight-cut dress.

Allegra had a natural instinct for determining different trends for each season. According to her, the latest winter season meant sweaters and tracksuits were definitely out.

Sometimes I would dispute this. "But its winter. It's freezing."

She'd object. "But Angelina Ballerina doesn't wear sweaters. Princesses don't wear sweaters."

Curse you, Cinderella and Snow White! Curse You!

So what was in fashion last winter? According to Allegra, anything strapless, off the shoulder, netted, or see-through was definitely in. Swimwear was the season must-have.

Once, on a very cold day, I dressed Allegra for ballet. She was crying because she refused to wear the long-sleeved top. She entered the class with it on and come out without it.

"Did you ask the teacher to take it off?"

"Yes. I also told her I like to wear my ballet clothes like this." Allegra demonstrated by dropping her leotard off the shoulder. "Or like this." She then removed the sleeves, bearing a strapless top.

If this was what she was wearing at age three, what would she be wearing clubbing?

Allegra was very specific about summer trends.

When it came to summer fashion, particularly in sweltering summer heat, thick woollen stockings were a necessity. Skivvies were also good. Layers and layers of clothes were the trend.

Summer must-have items:

Thick skivvies

Woollen stockings

ALLEGRA'S FASHION TIPS

Winter must-have items:

Anything strapless or off the shoulder

Swimwear

Fresh flower accessories were also in. Especially in the hair or ear. But don't think tucking it behind the ear with bobby pins will suffice. According to Allegra's rules, you need to shove the entire stem down your ear canal. I caught her doing this once with confidence.

"This is how it's done, Mommy."

Haute Couture

Allegra's haute couture collection was an assembly of over-the-top tulle dresses which ranged from ballerina dresses to the entire cast of Disney ensembles. She wasn't so kind to her actual Disney princess dolls and Barbies.

Sheldon would say, "I feel sorry for them. They never have any clothes on."

Allegra would hand her naked doll to me, asking in a pleasant voice, "Mommy, can you please hold my Barbie?"

"Of course, sweetie."

Before I had the chance to touch the doll, Allegra would scream, "By the neck!"

Sorry. I didn't realize handling Barbie meant keeping her hostage.

Friends donated their outgrown princess outfits. She fell in love with one particular Snow White costume. It was meant to be for a ten-year-old, so it was over-the-top for a three-year-old, like an outfit from "My Big Fat Gypsy Wedding." She wore it 24 hours a day for about three days straight, including sleep time. Going to the restroom was cumbersome. Since she refused to take it off, I tucked the layers of bouffant into a ball. She looked like she was swallowed by a giant marshmallow sitting on the toilet seat.

Her love for big dresses led to dramas at the shopping center. One time, a nice store owner allowed Allegra to try on a princess gown. She didn't want to remove it and stormed out of the store, to the owner's disbelief.

Sheldon and I took action. "You grab her feet. I'll grab her hands."

It was quite a scene. She was flying horizontally in the air like super girl, with Sheldon and me pulling her from both directions. I tried to get the dress off, but Allegra was gripping it like it was super-glued to her fingers. The store owner's eyes were mortified and, once again, we had an audience waiting for the outcome.

Allegra screamed. "No! I don't want to take it off," and we almost ripped the dress. Fortunately, it was rescued tear-free and returned safely to the hanger. *Mental note: Do not pass by princess shops.*

I also matched her birthday cakes with her Disney muses.

For her third birthday, I spent hours decorating a Tinkerbell cake and months sculpting the accessories. When I finally did the big reveal, Allegra responded with melodramatic tears. They weren't tears of happiness.

"Give me back my fairies!"

Sheldon held her back like a bouncer does in a pub when a drunk person is about to take a swing at another person. I covered my arms over the cake and we managed to get her under lockdown. The cake was saved.

But there were repercussions. She uninvited me that night.

"You're not invited to my party, Mommy."

"Oh, yeah? Who's making your little party, princess?"

"Umm..."

I won that round. Eventually, I was granted readmission. The next day, when I glanced the other direction, she attacked the cake.

"You forgot this fairy, Mommy." STAB!

Sheldon and I yelled, "NO!"

Fortunately, she stabbed the little fairy in an aesthetically pleasing spot. Phew.

Shoe fetish

Allegra had a shoe fetish like Imelda Marcos. She loved them more than I did, particularly high heels. She'd go through my wardrobe, pick the sparkly heels, and clunk around the house.

"Watch out. You might fall."

"I won't fall."

She sustained a few head injuries just from the high heels alone. But, like a true fashionista, she'd get back onto that horse – or in this case, heels.

Once, in a shoe store, a brilliant pair of adult-sized pink glitter shoes was on display.

She was in awe. "Wow."

I don't know why I showed her. She threw a Starfish on the floor because she wanted me to buy them, not willing to listen to pragmatic advice like they weren't her size.

Fortunately, I found a similar toddler version in Kmart. She wore them in the sandpit every day and the sparkles fell off, lightly dusting her sandcastles.

Allegra's reactions to shoes reminded me of grown women's reactions, like the characters on "Sex and the City." Once, I bought her three pairs of Kmart shoes and lay them on the living room floor. When Allegra entered the room, her eyes lit up.

"Hurray!"

It was as though she had collected a pair of Jimmy Choos, Manolo Blahniks, and Christian Louboutins.

I was exacerbated with the fashionista battles. She was like a fashion queen on steroids.

I remember when I attended a baby shower, and watched the mother-to-be glow with the expectant news of a daughter. I said softy, "Does she know what she is getting herself into?"

A lady next to me knew what I was talking about and remarked, "Look how happy she is. Let's not burst her bubble."

Even my sister changed her mind and expressed her desire to have a baby. Sheldon and I looked at her incredulously.

"Do you seriously want one? Haven't you seen Allegra?"

"Yes, but my baby won't be like Allegra. Mine will be perfectly behaved by remote control."

My mother asked her where she planned to get her baby.

My sister replied, "eBay."

Zoolander

A true fashionista would not be complete without accompanying modeling poses.

Allegra really started developing her runway poses after she turned three. She knew how to strike a pose. She knew how to swing her hips and hold it. She knew how to stick her little tush out and admire it from the mirror.

Once, I asked to take a photo of her. Like a reflex, she stepped into modeling position number one within a micro-second. A series of flashes followed until she raised her palm,

"I'm done."

She was a true Linda Evangelista who knew when I was pushing into overtime.

She had a collection of poses and would notify me when she'd perfected the latest one.

"Mommy, do you want to see the latest pose I've been practicing in the mirror?"

I suppose that was "Blue Steel." She poked her bottom out, polishing her bum round and round with her hand in admiration.

"This is my new pose, Mommy."

"What are you modeling? Air freshener for farts?"

Red Carpet Fashion

After a while, I found it increasingly difficult to towel dry her after a shower.

"Don't touch my towel because it's my gown."

I'd watch in disbelief as she arranged her towel into a floor-length, strapless, red-carpet dress. She'd then pose and admire herself in front of the mirror. One time, she blew up at me because I disrupted the drape of her towel so her red carpet train didn't extend.

"You ruined it! It has to come out. It has to come out."

Make sure my dress goes out.

To be red-carpet ready, Allegra also needed her makeup. It went against my very moral fiber. I always thought I'd be strict and say no makeup until she was 16, but it was fighting the tsunami again.

There were days when Allegra and I played tug of war over make-up brushes to the point where the brush would be quivering in equilibrium, with equal force pulling in both directions. I don't know how the pint-sized child would win.

You couldn't trick Allegra.

If she asked for eye shadow and I pretended to dab some on her eyes, she'd shout, "Hey, there's nothing there!"

So I'd have to apply the real thing. With her soft baby skin, make-up just wouldn't stick. I must have had enough grooves and wrinkles to hold the pigment in. So I'd humor her by putting a tiny bit of green eye shadow on her eyes.

After approval, she'd say, "Thank you very much, Mommy. Now my eyebrows."

The day care teacher noticed her fondness for makeup, telling me, "Do you know Allegra talks to me about makeup like she's a twenty-year-old? We have conversations about it all the time. She tells me, 'Love your eyelashes. Love your eye shadow. I love the color of your lipstick.'"

Sometimes Allegra even judged my red carpet fashion, like she was Perez Hilton. I know there are a lot of sweet children in the world who say the nicest compliments to their parents. Allegra was not one of them. That's why when she did, I cherished it that much more.

We were driving to a wedding five hours away so I prepared my makeup and hair in the car.

Allegra looked at me and said the rare words, "Mommy, you look beautiful, like a princess."

I was touched. "Really? Like Cinderella?"

Allegra paused, thought about it for a moment and said, "Nah. Not that pretty."

At least she was blunt about it.

Bridezilla

There were two basic functions Allegra learned from an early age: how to breathe and how to become a bridezilla.

Anything was suitable – the tea towel, a skirt, even a curtain. Often at hotels and people's houses, I'd catch her standing metres from the window with the curtain draped around her head like a veil, still attached to the wall.

"I'm getting married."

"Who would you marry?"

"You, Mommy."

She tried to kiss me. Not a mother-daughter kiss, but a "Basic Instinct" style kiss.

I held her back. "What are you doing?"

"This is how it goes, Mommy. One head goes on top and one head goes on the bottom." She twisted my head on an angle.

My friends responded, "What are you showing her on TV?"

I was showing Allegra Disney movies and this was what she was learning – French kissing.

It then hit me. Who would marry Allegra? She could only handle boys at day care who didn't fight back. That was the feedback from the teachers. She liked kids she could push around and interrogate.

Kiss me, Mommy. One head goes on top and the other head goes on the bottom, just like in "Rapunzel."

One time, I showed Allegra a Taylor Swift music video, "Love Story," thinking she'd enjoy the princess story. Instead, she had about 50 questions.

"Why's he late?"

"Why did the prince not come?"

"Why's he making her wait for him?"

"Why's he still not coming?"

"Why's he taking so long?"

I thought, good luck, Mr. Future Boyfriend of Allegra. You have a lot to be accountable for.

I pictured Allegra with a lasso, hunting an unsuspecting man, tying him up, and marrying him. Poor guy. But, then again, Sheldon and I would finally gain our freedom from Allegra. He'd live.

I decided it would be cute if I bought Allegra a kids "Getting married" costume when she was two. Within minutes of placing it on her head in the parking lot, she was having a colossal fit, flicking her hair left and right.

"This is NOT how it goes. This veil is not meant to be touching my ears!"

Watch out. There's a toddler bridezilla on the loose in Sydney.

At one stage, she demanded a "royal wedding." It must have been when Kate and Wills were married. I had to be resourceful, so I grabbed the biggest bed sheet I could find, placed her tiara on her head, and snapped a photo. She enjoyed her royal garb and completed it with a wave. That was, until she had a toilet training accident on her royal sheets. She passed it over to me.

"I'm all done, Mommy. I'm going to play blocks now."

I was left to deal with the royal damages.

Have another one

Sheldon and I eventually grew to love Allegra and our new roles as parents. (You can find out how in the next chapter.) We made it through our initiation, so it was time for the next big question on everyone's lips: "Are you going to have another one?"

Allegra put in her request. "I want one older brother and two younger sisters."

I turned to Sheldon. "You'd better be the one to explain why an older brother may be a bit of a challenge."

Even the day care teacher asked me to have another one so she could keep it. It sounded like a great entrepreneurial idea. I could pop out extra versions of Allegra, and sell them on eBay.

My mother offered prize money for a baby brother or sister for Allegra.

I turned towards her. "Why would you want another one when babysitting is such a sacrifice? I don't want to have another one because I want to keep my lupus manageable."

My mother simply replied, "What if I adopt Allegra and I can give her back when she's older?"

Allegra and my mother? That would be the clash of the titans.

Sheldon was 97% certain he didn't want another child, and I was 96% certain. I may have fluctuated 1-2% whenever I got clucky with friends' babies. A simple scream would bring me back to my 96% reality mark.

Friends told me, "Your second child will be the opposite."

I would have believed that if it wasn't for the experience of one friend.

She said, "People told me the second would be the opposite, you know, much easier. So I had another child, and he turned out to be worse. He was more challenging!"

I knew it was a slim chance, but with our luck, we would have been that 1%. We couldn't take the risk. I also wanted to manage my lupus.

So, in January 2012, we happily welcomed our second child. We announced her arrival on Facebook and received many messages.

"Congratulations!"

"We are so happy for you."

"You've been waiting a long time."

Our new baby is self-sufficient. She's always ready for all seasons, wears the most luxurious leather, doesn't need makeup, nail polish or veils, is always perfectly poised, and is content being in our presence. Even Allegra loves her comfy hugs.

We all get along with our new baby. She's our brand new couch. Her name is Delta B. Garcia.

"B" is for Burger King.

And she is so obedient.

PART II

Parents' Survival Kit

Don't get angry at me and I won't get angry at you!

Chapter 15

Rescue Remedies

By now, you probably think I'm a great survivor or a completely crazy woman who should be locked up for my anti-child ranting. But, all jokes aside, there were actually steps that helped me not only survive the challenging baby and toddler phase, but eventually thrive into parenthood. In particular, I noticed the biggest changes occurred when I started studying to become a life coach, and I applied some of the strategies that I suggested to clients.

Little steps, such as valuing myself enough to take some personal time out for me, helped to improve my wellbeing and the way I reacted to Allegra. Other steps, such as simply getting involved in my own projects, like starting a business or a hobby, renewed my feeling of self-worth. Thanks to my coaching teacher, Sandy Forster, I started a gratitude journal. This did wonders by increasing my appreciation for all the blessings in my life – even if my blessing was in the form of a demanding, bra-wearing toddler bridezilla.

I found by taking time to breathe deeply and contemplate the entertainment and laughter Allegra brought into our lives, I felt more balanced and at peace. After all, if Allegra was chuckling in the house and able to devise grandiose schemes, we must have been doing all right.

I learned this the day that I took time out to reflect and contemplate in a church full of people. I was pondering deeply, thanking God for such a blessing, when a male stranger tapped me from behind.

"Excuse me. You have a bib Velcroed to your back."

Of all bibs, why did it have to be the tattered, stained bib complete with threads hanging, on public display?

He tried to reassure me. "It happens all the time."

Somehow, I found that very hard to believe.

Life is a miracle, children are miracles, and the fact that you are still alive after they have shuffled your life around is also a miracle. Children add the "chocolate salt" to your life, making it far more interesting than it was before.

Allegra still drives me crazy, but after the sand settles from the diva sandstorm, I can't help but feel, "I love my cheeky little monkey."

If you find yourself covered in a little too much chocolate salt, I suggest trying one or more of these tips that helped me.

TIP 1 – BE KIND TO YOURSELF

It is so easy to put yourself down as a new parent when the internet and other media portray unrealistic salon-styled flawless parents. Perhaps even the "perfect parent" projection in your mind doesn't match your reality.

So you weren't that patient, super-hero perfect mother or father you were expecting. So you weren't able to breastfeed as society expects. So you weren't able to stay at home and look after the kids full-time because of work. Did the world crumble? No.

The truth is, you are an amazing parent and worthy of being loved just as you are. This includes whether you are sleep deprived and in a crappy mood venting your frustrations to the world, or quietly cradling your child in your arms radiating with love. Give yourself permission to be you.

Accepting yourself as a parent only during the "positive" times is a fantasy. Everybody has positive and negative moments. You are patient and impatient, happy and angry, strict and lenient, and so forth. These "negative" traits you may try to hide, serve an important purpose in raising your child. Growing up, my mother sometimes appeared to be "angry" or "cruel" to keep me safe, teach me a lesson, or encourage responsibility and independence. Today I thank her for this. So value every part of yourself.

Reduce Self-Criticism

If you find that you are putting yourself down more than lifting yourself up, start by reducing the negative self-talk.

Instead of saying "I suck as a parent," or "I'm the worst parent in the world," try to balance this by finding evidence in your life where you are doing a great job raising your child.

How have you provided love, shelter, food, or warmth for your child? Once you let self-criticism go, half your battle is gone.

Begin saying a simple affirmation. For example, "Even though I lose my patience, I love and fully accept myself," or "Even though I'm not coping as well as I hoped and am sometimes a psycho parent, I love and fully accept myself." Speak honestly from your reality and add "I love and fully accept myself."

If you can, stand in front of the mirror and affirm yourself. It may be confronting, but it allows you to face yourself and heal. Louise Hay taught me the importance of mirror work in her books "You Can Heal Your Life,"[1] and "The Power is Within You."[2] You are doing a great job raising your child. Ultimately, all your child needs is your love.

Affirm yourself with love

"I love and accept myself through joys and challenges."
"I may not be perfect, but I'm everything to my child."
"Even though I feel limited, I love and approve of myself."
"Even though I am far from perfect, I am perfect in my imperfections."

You can receive free bonus affirmations from my website: www.valuelifecoaching.com

Don't forget to give your child permission to have perfections and imperfections. Sounds stupid? Not really. Although I'm sure many people hate to admit it, there can be challenging times when parents think, "You ruined my sleep," or "You took away my life," or "You won't stop crying! Why are you making my life so difficult?"

---

1   Hay, Louise L. *You Can Heal Your Life.* Carlsbad, CA: Hay House, Inc., 1984.

2   Hay, Louise L. *The Power Is Within You. Carlsbad,* CA: Hay House, Inc., 1991.

Try to find the ways your child brings you joy.

You may say, "You test me, yet your smile brings me happiness."

"You take away my sleep yet bring adventure into my life."

Speak from your heart.

As you learn to love and accept your baby as a reflection of you, with perfections and imperfections, you can begin to enjoy the parenting journey.

TIP 2 – DON'T COMPARE YOURSELF

What a boring place this world would be if all parents were the same. You are unique, and your child is unique. No two thumbprints are the same, so why should parenting be the same?

I put myself through so much suffering by comparing myself to other mothers from Wisteria Lane. It made my challenging journey even heavier. Although some people are fortunate enough to have easy-going babies, you never know what challenges they may be experiencing in other areas of their lives.

Also, some people feel comfortable sharing all their struggles (like me), while others prefer to share with close friends. So it's really wasted energy comparing yourself to others because you don't really have the full picture. It's better to invest your energy enjoying the present moment and celebrating your unique relationship.

What about the aunties, parents, friends and acquaintances who insist their way of parenting is the best way? Just say, "Thank you," and leave it at that. Try it and if it doesn't work, move on.

I used to get worked up when I found the same techniques my friends were using just didn't have the same effect on my toddler. Instead of suffering in the naughty corner, she'd beg to go there like it was her secret garden.

Once sentenced, I often found her sunbathing in the naughty corner. I even tried spanking her, since that seemed to have worked on us. Allegra simply learned she could spank back. Sometimes, we'd be spanking each other like a BFF fight.

Some people told me, "It's because you aren't following the steps," but I found Allegra was just different.

I gave up on everyone else's tips and worked out a system that worked best for Allegra and me.

TIP 3 - RELEASE ALL YOUR ANGER, FRUSTRATION, OR RESENTMENT IN A SAFE WAY

Sometimes it is just darn hard to think positively when you are caught up in a sea of exasperating emotions and your hormones are on a roller coaster. That is why this tip can help pave the way for the rest of the tips in the survival kit.

Release your emotions, don't bottle them up

You don't have to be a hero by burying all those frustrations, anger, or negative feelings deep inside so you to appear to be coping or are more socially acceptable. Bottling and suppressing negative feelings inside your body can lead to bigger meltdowns, or make you physically sick in the future. Louise Hay discusses this in her book "The Power is Within You."[3]

The secret is to find safe ways to release these emotions or channel them out of your body.

These were the strategies that helped me:

1. Find a non-judgemental friend, or a friend who has been through a similar experience as you, and vent in person, or over the phone, all your feelings without worrying about editing them. But set a limit; for example, 10 minutes. After you get it out of your system, move on. Don't remain in the negative cycle of thoughts.

---

3. Hay, Louise L. *The Power Is Within You*. Carlsbad, CA: Hay House, Inc., 1991.

2. Go into a room, close the doors and windows, and scream into a pillow, yelling all your frustrations. Get all that energy out of you. You will feel more peaceful afterwards and more equipped to care for your baby.

3. If you have the opportunity, do some physical activity. Go for a brisk walk, jog, or run with the stroller. Or go to the gym and exercise, or dance to release the anger. Sometimes I used the built up energy to declutter parts of our home. I always felt better afterwards.

4. Write out your frustrations on a piece of paper, and then throw it away. Alternatively, writing in a journal is a great way to channel those feelings. I know it helped me.

5. See a professional counsellor.

I will expand on some of these tips further as you read on. By releasing these emotions in a safe way, you will be more peaceful, rather than being highly charged when handling your baby. It creates space for more positive energy to flow into your life.

TIP 4: YOUR GREATEST CHALLENGE IS YOUR GREATEST SUCCESS

In my introduction, I mentioned the impact Dr. Demartini had on my life. In his book, "Inspired Destiny,"[4] he describes how what you perceive to be your biggest challenge and what you think is blocking you from living out your purpose is, in fact, the very thing you need to achieve your inspired destiny.

For years, I believed that Allegra, and all the challenges that came packaged with her, was preventing me from living out my dreams and goals. I couldn't think straight with her dramas, let alone go for my own dreams. Dr. Demartini taught me a new belief system. He helped me understand that challenges exist to help us "on" our way

---

4. Demartini, John F. *Inspired Destiny: Living a Fulfilling and Purposeful Life.* Carlsbad, CA: Hay House, Inc., 2010.

to our higher-evolved self, and are not "in" the way. But this depends on whether you ask the right set of questions. So I asked myself:

"How did my greatest challenge – Allegra – help me achieve my purpose in life?" instead of questioning how Allegra prevented me.

I asked, "How did she give me life?" instead of rambling about how she took my life away.

Everything I viewed as a setback, I turned around into an asset.

"How did her tantrums serve me?"

"How did her drama serve others?"

"How was her inability to sleep an asset?"

I came up with a list of benefits. Without experiencing Allegra, in all her Hollywood glory, I may not have had the desire and drive to pursue becoming a life coach. Her alertness and inability to sleep meant she was taking in the world and learning very fast, which meant I could converse with her at an early age. Her tantrums taught me to be authoritative and allowed me to exercise patience. Her diva-ness provided laughter to the world. She taught me how to love at a deeper level. Without her drama, I wouldn't have a book to write.

What are the benefits?

Try asking yourself how any apparent parenting setback has benefitted you or others. How has this character trait served the world?

If you find this difficult, just visualize your child in the future all grown up, doing something extraordinary with that very thing you found challenging. When they win the Nobel prize because of all your hard work, you can also claim half the prize.

TIP 5: DISCOVER THE SPECIAL "SPARK" IN YOUR CHILD

Every child is extraordinary. Every child has their own special "spark." Take the time to look for it. It may be the way they laugh, dance, or smile. As I mentioned in the last tip, I thought Allegra's high maintenance diva-ness was the slow death of my life, but it was this special something that made life more interesting.

I now have people trying to book their chiropractic adjustments in the same timeslot as mine just to meet the little star of my stories. I don't know if I would have had the same reception with my fantasy soccer-playing son.

List your child's special qualities

Instead of thinking about the list of things that are frustrating, ask yourself, "What are the special qualities my child has?" Write a list. It may range from artistic or sporting abilities to simply being able to provide comfort by giving you a hug.

You may even extend this activity to finding the extraordinaire in you. What are your star qualities as a parent?

TIP 6: HUMOR CURES EVERYTHING

I've heard laughter has the power to cure even cancer. In the midst of a parenting crisis, sometimes Sheldon and I would just recap stories and laugh.

I truly got through the terrible twos by sharing stories with friends. In Allegra's case, I posted her daily antics on Facebook. Somehow, knowing it amused others made the whole situation easier to bear.

Share your funny stories

When the going gets tough, particularly during the newborn stage, teething, and the terrible twos, think about something cute or funny your child has done, and share it with one other person. You are improving their day and shifting your own energy around. Your child will also become more settled when you have had a good laugh.

Allegra often switched into laughter in the middle of a tantrum, in reaction to my laughter. I can't help but laugh whenever she does that dramatic "The Notebook" tanty.

If you feel game, share your story or photos with the world on Facebook, Twitter, or Pinterest.

You can even write your own collection of stories through a blog, keep the stories to give to your child later in life, or even publish a book.

Who knows? Someone may make a movie out of it. I know Allegra is considering Kim Kardashian to play her role.

Watch a comedy

If you can't think of anything your child does that makes you smile (which I find hard to believe), go and watch a funny movie or television show. I survived watching episodes of "Seinfeld" and "Glee."

TIP 7: REINVENT YOURSELF

One of the reasons I felt depressed when Allegra was born was because I felt I no longer owned my own life. It belonged to someone else. I knew in my head that while I was losing my former life, I was gaining something greater – the experience of motherhood. Nevertheless, a part of me still felt restless.

Not everyone feels this way, and I know some people feel even more complete after having a baby. Regardless of whether you do or don't relate, just because a baby is completely dependent on you, it shouldn't stop you from doing something exciting for yourself.

Create something new, or do what you love

You may want to take up a hobby, return to an old interest, start a project or finish a project, start a blog, or even start a small business.

I had friends that began making and selling jewelery when their babies were born. I had other friends who purchased sewing machines and began creating items of value to sell. One of my friends decided to pursue her master's degree and Ph.D. after having a baby. Another enrolled in a new university course.

You could reinvent yourself. What would you love to do?

I decided to feed my brain by studying an online course with the Inspired Spirit Coaching Academy to become a life coach.

Do it at your own pace, when you feel ready

It doesn't matter what it is, as long as you do something that fulfils you. It may take some time, but as long as you do it at a pace you are comfortable with, it's fine.

I know mothers who started their projects as soon as their babies were born, while others, like myself, waited until their children were old enough to go to day care. One of my friends decided to do a career change and train to be a pilot, after her two children started primary school. She officially completed her first supervised take off and was happy to share this news.

Even if you do return to your former workplace, taking pleasure in doing something you love is always beneficial.

I believe we are always expanding ourselves, always growing. If we weren't changing, we would simply be dead.

Dr. John Demartini taught me that your life's vitality is a reflection of your level of inspiration.

So if you feel like you've been robbed of life, or if you simply want to explore new possibilities, pursue something that inspires you, no matter how small it may be. Doing this restores self-worth and gives you an identity again so you are not just a food supply or diaper changer.

TIP 8: SEEK PROFESSIONAL HELP

There is a huge range of help available. Don't be afraid to ask for it. You are not a weakling and contrary to some perceptions, there is nothing wrong with you or your baby. They are simply there to help you and your baby become more of a team. Some people were against me seeking help. They felt it confirmed I was a bad mother and something was wrong with my child. This is far from the truth.

As I mentioned earlier, I must have dealt with all the nurses in Sydney along my journey. Some of them were great, many were extraordinary, and one or two looked at me like I was an alien. Nevertheless, I kept asking for help. I would have never made it without them.

When I struggled, nurses referred me to free settling programs or workshops. I also did a baby massage course and a terrible twos seminar.

There are various organizations that focus on feeding and settling techniques. In Sydney, organizations such as Karitane or Tresillian do day appointments, as well as a live-in program. There are counselors available who can help with the baby blues. I found this service particularly helpful.

There are charity organizations that have volunteers come into your home and relieve you for a few hours a week. You can contact your local health center, doctor, or hospital to find out about special programs or organizations available in your area.

TIP 9: GET OUT AND ABOUT

If you get a serious case of talking to the walls and inanimate objects, you know you need to get out of the house!

Toddlers love exploring the world. Allegra would run for miles, like she was itching to stretch her legs after being couped up at home.

It's amazing how beneficial strolling outside, walking barefoot on grass, or going to the beach can be. Breathe in some fresh air and do little bit of exercise by pushing the stroller outdoors or letting your child run free under your supervision. Start mixing with people at your local park, enjoy the sunshine, and stare at the clouds.

I remember when I was in the middle of a crisis and we went to Bondi Beach. Just feeling the sea breeze and watching the waves crash into the ocean was enough to heal me.

TIP 10: CATCH UP WITH YOUR GIRLFRIENDS, OR MANFRIENDS, OR JOIN A MOTHERS' GROUP

Take some time to have coffee with your close friends who are in the same boat. There are a number of child-friendly cafes or indoor play centers that can be found in your area. You can search for them online. These have enough toys and books to keep the tiny ones busy so you can engage in adult conversation.

Your local health center can direct you to a mothers' group, or you can form your own group with local mothers or close friends. Some mothers organize their partners to babysit so they can get together child-free and do some pampering, like visiting a day spa. This leads me to my next tip.

TIP 11: HAVE SOME 'ME' TIME

Cheryl Richardson taught me the importance of 'me' time through her book, "The Art of Extreme Self-Care."[5] Do an activity for yourself once a week that's not work-related. Take a hot bath, watch a good movie, read a book, go to a day spa, put on makeup, or have a photoshoot. You can join a meditation class or a dance class.

---

5. Richardson, Cheryl. *The Art of Extreme Self-Care* (2nd ed.). Carlsbad: Hay House, Inc., 2011.

In Sydney, new mothers receive a bag full of goodies and offers from the hospital. I took advantage of the free Napoleon Yummy Mummy makeover and organized a photoshoot with Allegra by using another free voucher.

When Allegra was finally in day care, I took the opportunity to get massages now and then. It made a world of difference. I also enjoyed taking dance lessons with my friend. Meditation really centred me and gave me a lot of peace.

Gyms and swimming centers also allocate a time with free child sitting. You can call your local centers to find out what is available.

TIP 12: GO ON A DATE

Rekindle your relationship by taking some time out with your partner child-free. It may mean organizing it four months in advance, or paying for babysitting, but it is worth it.

If you can, make an effort to feel your sexy best. Making the effort to dress nicely increases your vibration or energy, and makes you feel more positive about yourself.

If you are too rushed to get dressed up, wear your favorite clothes and enjoy your time together. Just don't have a Velcro bib attached to your back.

I remember having my first five-minute date with Sheldon over a coffee. It felt like we hadn't spoken to each other in months. As conversations center all around the baby, it's worthwhile touching base, seeing how both of you are, and enjoying each other's company.

TIP 13: PUT YOUR CHILD IN DAY CARE, FAMILY CARE OR PRESCHOOL

If you can, give yourself some time off by putting your child into day care, family care, or preschool. Children get exposed to all sorts of fun learning experiences. Allegra has activities like hand-painting or bread-making; activities that I wouldn't allow her to do in our home because of the mess they make.

Children love to copy each other, so it makes teaching them some skills easier, like feeding, putting away toys, and toilet training. They learn to socialize and make friends.

If you choose not to send them to day care, family care, or pre-school, that's fine, as well. These tips are what helped me, and everyone is different. Try what resonates with you.

TIP #15: ASK A HIGHER SPIRITUAL POWER TO HELP YOU

When it gets tough, ask God, higher consciousness, Universal power, the Universe or whatever you like to call it to help you. I used to pray, "You gave me this miracle baby. Now give me the miracle strength to raise her." Other times, I simply prayed, "Why? Why? Why?" The Universe gives you exactly what you need to grow. It may throw challenges at you, to teach you patience, or how to love unconditionally. You've been given exactly the circumstances you need to evolve into a better version of you. In the difficulties, take heart in knowing there is a master plan and that big mastermind behind it all has got your back.

If you think you aren't getting any answers, look around you. Sometimes your answer comes through that extra little bit of inner strength. Other times, it may come through a friend willing to listen to you. Sometimes you need to take action in order to see the help. When times get stressful and crazy, just let go and say, "I trust in God, the Universe, in a higher power, and I am safe everywhere in the universe."

TIP 16: CONSIDER OTHER FORMS OF CHILDREN

There are benefits in going through the whole process again by having more children. Your first child gets to have siblings to play with, and the relationships developed are priceless.

Just know that if you choose not to go down this path again, there are always other forms of children. Ignore how others judge you. I've been told everything from "Good on you!" to "I can't believe you are robbing Allegra of a sibling! You are robbing her of experiences." But I also learned from Dr. Demartini that there is neither gain nor loss, only transformation. Whatever she misses in one form is compensated by another form. She may not have experienced the joy of siblings, but she has experienced travel adventures and the joy of meeting family and friends from all over the world. One experience is not better or worse than another. It is just different.

Our second child, Delta our couch, is much easier to bear. Pieces of furniture, a car, a plant, or a pet may be easier options than siblings. Give them a funky name. Consider this the other option.

If you have any questions regarding implementing these tips, or would like to some one on one help by collaborating with me as your life coach, contact Anna by email anna@valuelifecoaching.com

Chapter 16

Parents from around the world share what helped them through the tough times

Don't like my tips? Don't worry. They are not for everyone. That's why I've asked parents from around the world to share what got them through the insane or most challenging moments in parenthood. Even if you find yourself over getting advice, knowing others are going through the same experiences as you may give you that little bit of comfort.

Focus on the precious moments

"I had never changed a diaper prior to having a baby and I told anybody who asked that I would hire a nanny. It didn't work out that way. Those first three months were really tough on an uninitiated mom such as me.

My husband was even more clueless than I, and afraid of dropping and hurting the baby. So I took care of Kailyn twenty-four hours a day.

What got me through was knowing this tiny human being depended on me. Focusing on those precious moments when she would fall asleep on my chest and turn her head when she heard my voice also got me through. A little cake and ice cream and also did wonders."

KT, mother of one

Relax... crying is what babies do

"I remember when Nikolaus woke up in the middle of the night and wouldn't stop crying. My wife and I took turns trying everything to settle him. We were both exhausted and couldn't take anymore. In the midst of his screaming, we stared at each other and thought what we were doing was crazy. We were letting this little innocent baby get to us and were stressing over absolutely nothing!

Babies cry. That's what they do. We had to learn to disassociate the sound of crying from our own stress and anxiety. As soon as we learned to be calm and relaxed in the face of those cries, we found it easier to calm him. Babies can really sense stress, and it stresses them out, too!"

Nalee, father of two

Remember, babies grow up quickly

"During the tough times, what got me through was taking a slow, deep breath, remembering this was only momentary. Before I'd know it, they would be all grown up wanting their independence. I'd also say a short prayer for strength, patience, and love.

Alternatively, hiding in the walk-in pantry to get a few minutes of quiet time was another option (the toilets weren't safe anymore!)."

Bea, mother of three

Tag-team with your partner

"Siena and Lucas were not very good sleepers. Some major challenges we faced were getting enough sleep, managing the late night and early morning feeds, and re-settling. Teamwork with my wife was important to maximize our sleep.

216

Since Tracy was an early sleeper and I was a late sleeper, I fed and re-settled the baby up until around 1:00 a.m. so that Tracy could rest and take over until the early hours. Eventually, our bodies adjusted to five or six hours of interrupted sleep. Of course, now and then we need a recharge, but it's amazing how parents can manage with such little sleep."

Mario, father of two

It's okay to have a cry, too

"It's interesting that I'm still alive, because there have been moments when I've felt that I wouldn't make it through. With two children and one on the way, I had my fair share of tough moments. Lack of sleep, being pregnant, and placing high expectations on oneself also made me one very emotional woman.

Sometimes you just have to let yourself cry. That lets out a lot of the emotions and you can move on with what you need to do. At the end of the day, you do it all out of love, and they eventually stop crying!"

Anna, mother of two (soon to be three)

You don't have to know everything

"When my baby was just born, all the maids had gone on vacation so I was left washing diapers. My baby started crying and I cried with her. I realized the hilarity of it all and wised up.

The lesson I learned was that you don't need to know everything. Just grow with your child and together learn about life. Just give the best that you can to this precious life in your hands. Your child will discover your sense of humor and the simple joys in life."

Chiquit, mother of two

Have a fighting spirit

"Along the way, there were some tough times, like when Sarah was six months old and my mom was starting to lose her battle with cancer. I must admit that it was the kids who gave me the spirit to keep going. I knew that they needed me and hiding under a rock was not an option. From that point on, I just had a fighting spirit and nothing ever got too hard."

Rina, mother of three

Appreciate simple pleasures

"I found that having an appreciation for simple everyday pleasures helped keep my sanity in check. Having small goals every day, like getting to my mid-morning cuppa with a sweet treat, was a little indulgence, and something I always looked forward to after a long, broken night's sleep. Those 15 minutes are golden nuggets every day."

Arlyn, mother of one

Tomorrow's a new day

"We always end up laughing about the things the kids put us through. Every time I had a rough day with the kids, I'd think, 'Tomorrow's a new day. I can start fresh and be stress free.'

During other times, when I found it tough, Kayla or Jai would randomly do something precious, like give me a big hug or say, "I love you, Mommy." It's almost as though they knew I was having a rough day. Moments like these really made everything worth it."

Dianne, mother of two

Children are making memories

"Having three boys under three, it can get very demanding when they all need my attention. As simple as it sounds, I'd take a few deep breaths, then get on with it. You become good at multi-tasking pretty quickly.

I often found myself putting Bub in the stroller and propping his bottle with a hand towel, while feeding our toddler and finding something to occupy our three-year-old, while I also organized dinner.

I came across a sign that said, 'Excuse the mess, the children are making memories.' I remember this sign every time my lounge room is covered in toys and books!"

Jodi, mother of three under three

Ask for help

"On the day that my husband was going overseas for eight weeks, I came down with severe bronchitis. I didn't have the energy to care for my two-year-old son for a day, let alone the eight weeks. (Hats off to single parents who still manage when they're sick.) My parents came to visit and my mom ended up staying the whole week. When things get tough, it's a great big blessing to have parents you can depend on."

Nancy, mother of one

Turn up the music

"Well, when times got really tough, I would turn up the music, hype myself up, and just do what needed to be done. I believe every woman has inner strength. I love being a mom and I wouldn't have it any other way."

Nina, mother of four

Relax, you're doing a great job

"Not long after our second son was born, I said to my husband, 'Let me know if I'm stuffing this mommy thing up.' He replied, 'Do you still have two children?' I said, 'Yes.' 'Are they the same two children you left home with this morning?' 'Yes.' 'Then you are doing a great job.' That made me laugh."

Leesa, mother of two

Seek spiritual help

"I got together with other moms and prayed. That really helped a lot. We became a community that prayed for ourselves, each other, and other moms doing it tough. We also prayed for husbands and children. We still get together through the good times and the tough times of different stages of motherhood."

Cristina, mother of two

Do what works for you

"When my baby wouldn't fall asleep at night, I'd drive in the car until she fell asleep, or put her in bed with me.

People would tell me I shouldn't do this because she would never want to sleep in her own bed. I took the chance and, contrary to everyone's predictions, she eventually slept all night long in her own bed.

I realize that my parenting methods were far from ideal, but it was the best way I could do with such a demanding baby, who was soon off to school and is now 24."

Maria, mother of one

Take time out for yourself

"It was hard to take time out without the kids, as my husband worked long hours running our own business. But when the opportunity came up, I'd catch a movie or dinner with a friend.

During the times when this wasn't an option, I'd organize to go out with friends during the day, who also had small kids. We could vent while the kids played. It's great being able to talk to other like-minded moms about everyday issues and having a 'good whinge' and laugh!"

Selina, mother of three

"It's important to have some 'me' time, whether it be to go out with girl friends or to spend some time reading a good novel before going to sleep. That is my wind-down time."

Jovy, mother of three

Handling a tantrum

"When Bella was naughty or had a tantrum, she would go in her room until she finished crying (even if it took 30 minutes of carrying on and shouting). We would not open the door or give attention until she finished and spoke to us in calm manner. When she behaved, we rewarded her with lots of cuddles, praise, or a small present."

Ruth, mother of two

"When Mia would have a crying tantrum, we would give her a pacifier and take her to a quiet room, which had no distractions (mostly the bedroom), and lie down next to her until she calmed down."

Johnny and Annica, parents of one

It will get easier as they grow older

"When I was feeding my newborn Cody, I knew I had to keep my two-year-old Jesse occupied. I'd set up a small television with a DVD he enjoyed, or I'd ask him to help me, for example, by grabbing a diaper. When it got tough, I thought, it could only get easier as the boys got older. Now they get along really well, and I hope they become the best of mates."

Lucy, mother of two

Have date nights

"Sometimes I'd ask mom to watch the kids if I needed time out with Pete. I didn't want my marriage to be affected by my super busy kiddy life, and I didn't want Pete to feel that I was neglecting him. Sometimes it would be dinner, a short drive to get a frozen Coke, or watching a movie. If we couldn't get mom to watch the kids, there was always DVDs."

Lisa, mother of four

Communication is the key

"The most important thing is that both parents are on the same page with everything and work collaboratively to nurture a happy child. Communication is the key. It's important that the child knows and understands where you stand on things, like from what's wrong or right, appropriate behavior, and manners. Furthermore, stay calm, have lots of patience, and be a good listener. Have plenty of praises and endless love to give."

Rhodora, mother of one

Stick to your guns!

"If you say no – then stick to it, even though you will get the whining and crying. Sometimes you feel really, really bad. Tough love is always hard, but it will surely pay off. I have always stuck to that and my kids know that once mommy says no, it's no! By doing this, they remember you are in control and not them."

Jess, mother of three

As they grow up, show them who's boss

"Never let your children feel that they have power over you. This may seem like I'm a power-hungry parent, but the reality is most children will try to push you to see how far they can go. If you set your expectations early, you'll spend less time fighting them and more time enjoying one another!"

Tanja, mother of two (soon to be three)

"Remember that in order to raise them as pleasant, responsible, and smart adults, you as parents, need to treat them as one. They are still in training. You're the parent (trainer), and they're the child (trainee). Have fun growing up together! And, lastly, include Jesus (or a higher power you believe in) as your co-trainer and guide."

Maricet, mother of two

Cool down by asking your partner to step in

"Having a child is the best gift in the world. Nothing can replace the happiness, laughter, and love they give you.

When I'd have a bad day, I'd tell Mike to deal with the kids as soon as he got home, so I could cool down. Once I had a break for the night, I was energized again to give my all in taking care of them."

Ruth, mother of two

Kids will learn when they are ready

"I had my son when I was 19 years old and it was a challenge. Raising a kid when you are still a kid seems 100 times harder. Sleepless nights, potty training, tantrums, and the stresses of picky eating (to name a few) may have gotten the best of me. I was frustrated and angry. Potty training was a nightmare, and transitioning to solid food was near hopeless.

Everybody tells you that raising a child is not easy, but you never realize what that means until you get there. What helped me cope through the tough times was realizing kids will do what they want when they are ready. You do the best you can to encourage and guide, but it's still up to the little kid. Never use anger to get them to do what you want. Instead, take several deep breaths, say a little prayer, hug your child, and try again tomorrow."

Kristine, single mother of one

Do what feels right for you, your child, and your family

"Motherhood is like nothing you can imagine. You picture yourself bringing home a precious little baby from the hospital, and you are overwhelmed with all the dreams and hopes you have for yourself, your child, and your family. Personally, having three children five years and under is hectic, exhausting, and a blessing. It is so easy to lose yourself – you are the mother, wife, partner, housekeeper, cook, and so forth – but you have to remember who you are.

Our children will remember the stories shared, their exciting day trips or 'adventures' as labeled in our house, the laughs, kisses and cuddles, and the fun of being a kid. I have never heard someone thank their parent for having a spotless house during their childhood. Be kind to yourself, do what you feel is right for you, your child, and your family."

Sarah, mother of three

If all else fails …

"Birth control is your friend."
Maria, mother of two

PART III

Allegra's Greatest Hits

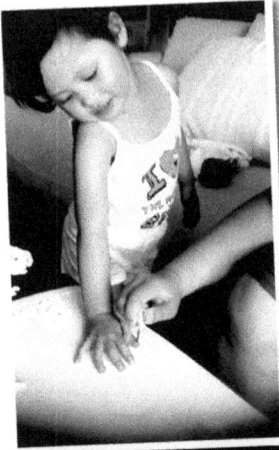

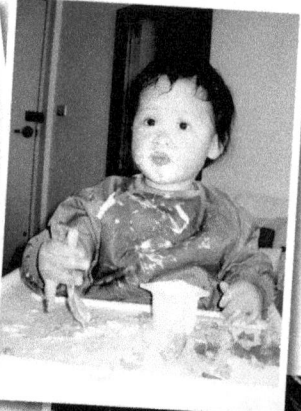

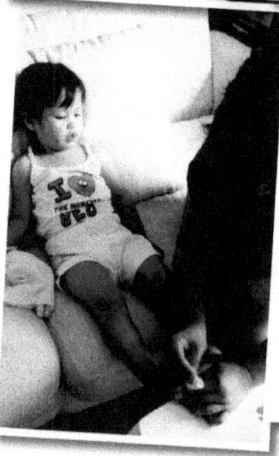

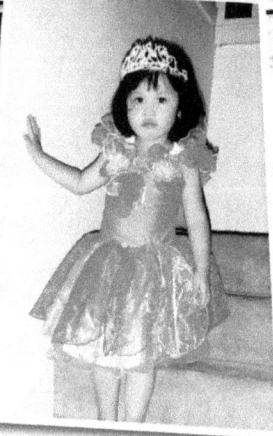

Chapter 17

The Golden Collection

The split-second pose

It has been quite a remarkable journey raising Allegra. The Universe wanted her to be in our lives for a reason, and now I have written about it. Through the ups and downs, Sheldon and I have learned to appreciate her uniqueness as a gift, particularly the entertainment she offers the world. Allegra has settled from her extravagant tantrums but continues to entertain us. There are many more facets of her personality, so I have compiled some of her stories into this chapter. I hope you enjoy it.

Allegra, Mommy and Daddy love you so much!

I found a massive amount of water all over the rug.

"Allegra!"

"I didn't do it, Mommy. The cup did it."

After a long, hard day, my father relaxed in an armchair and drank his beer. Allegra pointed to his beer gut and said her first word, "Baby."

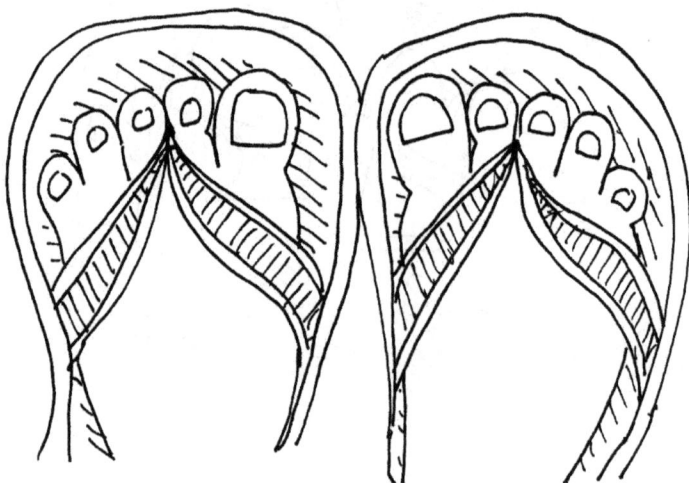

Allegra pays so much attention to detail when it comes to her footwear.

What does the duck say?

Quack quack.

What does the cow say?

Moo moo.

What does the pig say?

Oink oink.

What does the zebra say?

Cough cough.

I must have had the flu when I taught her the zebra.

I gave her a chocolate and said, "Only eat half because it's not good for your tummy."

Allegra blurted, "But it's good for my mouth!"

I gave her my best strict mommy face, but inside I was thinking, "That's a good comeback."

We took Allegra to the farm, thinking it would be a good educational experience. When we asked her to pose with the kangaroo, she jumped on the kangaroo, treating the poor animal like a ride.

Sorry, Allegra. I didn't realize the proper way to carry Barbie was to hold her hostage.

Allegra has so much love for people she doesn't remember.

I was removing Allegra's top to prepare for her shower. She started doing a crazy dance in her little white singlet (undershirt), singing: "All the single-lets, all the single-lets, all the sing-lets. Oh-oh-oh..." I might have to write to Beyonce about Allegra releasing the singlet version of "Single Ladies."

Allegra knew how to use her loud voice at the most appropriate times. While inside a public restroom stall, Allegra began singing loudly, "You do the hokey pokey and you... Mom, do you want me to wipe your bum?"

Apparently turning three gives you rights.

What do you do when your child has nightmares? I told Allegra that Mother Mary would sleep with her.

With a piercing look in her eyes, she responded with the most critical question, "But does she wear sparkly stockings?"

"Err... Yes."

When nature does not meet Allegra's expectations.

Every night, we went through the royal procedure. After showering, I brushed her hair and sang Disney's "Tangled" Rapunzel song. I even acted like her magic hair turned my gray hairs black. In reality, I had a throbbing headache from working overtime for the princess.

The children were rehearsing for their Christmas concert when the day care worker asked the kiddies, "What would you like Santa to give you for Christmas?"

Most children shouted, "Toys."

Allegra put her hand up and said, "I'd like Santa to give me a baby in my tummy."

I certainly did not want Santa to give her that present.

Allegra said her nightly prayer to avoid nightmares, "Mother Mary, thanks for letting me dream about fairies, butterflies, and buttons... and hummus."

For a moment, I almost added Greek dolmades to her dream request.

We started toilet training Allegra. Instead of going to the toilet, she congratulated Sheldon every time he finished in the bathroom by saying, "Good girl!"

I was a little hesitant about dropping Allegra at Sheldon's law firm to attend a course.

He told her, "Be very quiet. The people are working."

So what did she do? She sang them your typical children's nursery rhyme, by belting out her loudest rendition of Katy Perry's song "Waking Up in Vegas."

The lawyers stopped working. That probably cost them thousands of dollars, but she never was one to follow instructions.

Allegra wore her sparkly silver shoes and told me to watch her do ballet. I was surprised to see her go 'en pointe' and point her legs out while holding onto furniture.

"Where did you learn that?"

She answered, "Peppa Pig."

Never underestimate the power of a cartoon pig.

I picked up Allegra from day care. The staff member told me Allegra was hilarious. "Allegra put her hands on her hips, swinging them side to side, as she did a pageant walk in front of her friends.... with her pants down!"

I told Allegra to wash her hands after going to the day care restroom.

"I don't have to wash my hands. Princesses don't wash their hands because their dresses are too long!"

I spent the next few hours profoundly pondering and meditating on this question – Do Disney princesses wash their hands after using a toilet?

Allegra was pointing her finger at all the kids at day care and threatening them with full aggression. "Do you know Mother Mary? Do you know Mother Mary?"

She kept interrupting the teacher, who was trying to give a lesson about child protection.

"Allegra you can ask me anything once I finish teaching this."

Now every kid knows about Mother Mary, since Allegra basically pointed a gun to their heads. I'm sure Mother Mary appreciates aggressive marketing.

I was talking with a friend when Allegra asked if she could stick Christmas stickers on me. I allowed her, and I continued my conversation. When she finished, she called an audience over to view her masterpiece. I looked at my dress and was slightly embarrassed.

After being told by Allegra that I wasn't invited to her birthday party, I turned to her and said, "Oh, yeah? Who's organizing your little party, Princess?"

"Um..."

Mommy won this time, baby.

She obviously knew what I was looking for. When Allegra said her prayer before bed so she wouldn't have nightmares, she added, "And Mother Mary, please help mommy to find a parking spot."

While all the day care children obediently sat on the floor, Allegra stood on the table and made a huge announcement. "I'm throwing a party and you are all invited!" She must have had a VIP list because Sheldon and I did not make the cut.

Allegra got out of bed and stomped into the kitchen. She put one arm on her hip, and with one finger pointing at me she started telling me off for not buying replacement Band-Aids as I had promised. (She needs an endless supply for her invisible blood. I can never see anything on her apparent injuries.) She went on and on, and finished the lecture with so much angst, saying I was in deep, deep trouble.

When she left, Sheldon and I looked at each other. "What just happened?"

When it comes to traveling with Allegra, I never take my eyes off her. Although she's been on so many flights, traveling with her still makes me pull out my hair.

While I turned my head for a few seconds, I looked back to find Allegra wheeling away a stranger's huge suitcase from a check-in point. The woman ran after Allegra to get her bags back.

While I was collecting my baggage at the carousel, I turned my shoulder to find Allegra getting rid of my hand-carry items by loading them on the conveyor belt.

Getting on the plane, we held up the line. Allegra made herself comfortable on every seat in business class, saying, "I think I found my seat," "I think I found my seat," and then, "Oh, here it is."

The man seated there said to Allegra, "Nice try."

My sister said she'll think twice about traveling with us again.

There was one interesting observation. Allegra intently studied the evacuation process on the plane. Her eyes lit up when she saw the diagrams with the flotation gear. "Hurray! Are we going swimming on the plane, Mommy?" Let's hope not.

264

Finale

So what is parenthood really like?

There are plenty of fun adventures.

Plenty of opportunities to use your muscles.

And opportunities to enjoy your brand new
furniture in your designer home.

There are plenty of special dinners.

And plenty of action in the bedroom.

We wouldn't have it any other way.

Fin

About the Author

Anna Garcia is an author, life coach, illustrator, graphic designer, and mother. She has also enjoyed a fulfilling career as a visual arts teacher, and spent years doing full-time voluntary work.

Despite having lupus, Anna gave birth to her miracle daughter, Allegra, the muse of all her stories. Anna was inspired to start her own life coaching business to help other people transform their lives and achieve their goals.

Anna has a strong belief that any setback is a blessing in disguise. She chooses to share how she overcame her personal challenges of first-time parenting using coaching strategies, and now helps people all around the world through life coaching.

Her ultimate life goal is to inspire people to do what they are most passionate about.

Anna currently lives in Sydney with her husband, Sheldon, and daughter, Allegra.

You can contact Anna through anna@valuelifecoaching.com

Or visit her websites: www.valuelifecoaching.com

www.putthebabyback.com